Same Shit
Different Day

Breaking the Patterns that
Make us Miserable

A metaphysical approach to wellbeing

Paula O'Sullivan

Dedication

I dedicate this book to my lovely sons, Joshua & Matthew, I'm so blessed to have two amazing guys like you in my life. To the memory of my parents Lily & James (Paddy) & my brother Jimmy O'Sullivan, to my beautiful sisters Anna & Elaine, to my lovely niece Liz, and all my friends, you're the very best, and to all of you who have shared my journey so far, I wish you much love and light always, may you be blessed with the awareness of the Divine within you. Namaste xxx

Table of Contents

'No one changes unless they want to.
Not if you beg them. Not if you shame them.
Not if you use reason, emotion or tough love.
There's only one thing that makes someone change:
Their own realization that they need to do it.
And there's only one time it will happen:
When they decide they're ready'

Lori Deschene

Important Note for Readers

This book is not intended as a substitute for the advice of medical doctors or healthcare professionals etc. The reader should regularly consult a doctor in matters relating to their health and particularly with respect to any symptoms that may require diagnosis, medical attention or medication. The techniques shared are intended to be supplementary. The author and publishing platform are not responsible for any consequences occurring from the practice of anything discussed within these pages. Any application of the suggestions given are at the readers' discretion and is their sole responsibility.

Foreword

Welcome to my second book! This is a follow on from my first book, 'Different Perspectives for a Different World –Essays for Life' it was self-published in 2013 as a limited edition of only 200 copies. In 2017, I revised and re published it, making it available worldwide.

The first book was a collection of little philosophical essays that I wrote as I developed the ability to think for myself, I shared some tips in it to help, but I felt that I could maybe help further by writing a more detailed book about how I actually got myself healthy, freed myself of fears, anxiety and depression, and built my confidence and self-esteem.

For those of you who aren't familiar with my story, I'll briefly share it here. Back in 2009, I developed an MS / Lupus type illness. I discovered later that I had unconsciously created it through my reactions and responses to the stresses in my life. I subsequently began reading personal development, spiritual and metaphysical books. After practicing some techniques including self-hypnosis, mindfulness, CBT & NLP, I got better. Within three months most of my symptoms were gone, it took about eight months for my blood to return to normal.

Amazed at this, I wondered what else was possible. I left my husband, we had been together for 17 years and married for 13 of them. I had two young sons and we moved out of our house. I spent the following two years, working on myself, eliminating, fears, anxiety, depression, my excess weight and then I worked on building my confidence and self-esteem, and I started to create a new life for myself.

This led me into writing, and then I took back up my painting and drawing which I had given up on for 17 years. I took the T off can't, and realized that if I really wanted to do something then I would and could find a way to do it. I trained as a Hypnotherapist, Reiki Practitioner & compiled my first book out of the essays I had written over two years. I did all this while raising my two boys. No it wasn't easy.

People ask me how come I have done so much in the past 10 years. Well I stopped watching TV, listening to the radio, and reading newspapers. I realized when I had left my husband, just exactly how much time I had wasted. I was then 44. 'How much time would I have left to create a new life I asked myself?' No one can know the answer to such a question, so I decided to start right there and then to do what I could with what I had, and to do the best I could every day. I decided that the only things I would allow into my mind were those things that would help me to be a better person, and that when I learned something, that I would share it to help another.

In 2017, I qualified as a Life Coach. But I didn't get a chance to begin practicing that then in earnest as life threw another of its curveballs at me, which delayed the process just a little. So it's nearing the end of 2019 at the time of writing this and I'm creating a new life again. I have lots of plans! Someone once said 'We make plans and God laughs,' well I'm laughing too!

Just to say, life is going to keep testing you, and you may fall on your knees many, many times like I have, all I ask of you, is to promise me that you'll just keep getting back up every time!

So back to the contents of this book. It has all the tips and techniques that I used successfully on myself since 2009. I mention the books that were helpful and I've included a list at the end of this book of some recommended reading. All of those books I found invaluable, and still do. I often go back and re read them, there are always gems of information that reveal themselves the more I expand my consciousness.

Our lives would be so much easier if we knew that everything is energy, our thoughts, our emotions, our health, our wealth and our relationships.

Most of our misery is caused by our thoughts about things, and those thoughts create our feelings and emotions. Sounds so simple but unfortunately it's not. By being human we make it complicated!

I've broken the different areas into sections to make it easier to read and understand. But they are all connected to each other. Thoughts, emotions and energy come into everything.

I've had to repeat myself more than a few times, although I've tried to say the same thing a little differently where possible. This is to make it easier than having you leafing back and forth to find things I've said before. Mostly it is The Breathing Technique, The Two Ways of Thinking and Mind Movies, which I've duplicated, three essential practices if you want to change things in your life. I also included them at the end of the book for easy access. Mindfulness will get mentioned often too, as that's a life changer.

I'm sorry if this pisses you off, but after reading some of this book, you'll realize that it is your choice to be pissed off or to not be pissed off, it really hasn't anything to do with me! You don't have to believe everything I say here. Feel free to accept or reject anything. I encourage you to do your own research, then practice what you've learnt. Personal development is a process, the more you practice something, the better you get at it, that's been my experience anyway. There is no right or wrong way, only your way. Find a way that works for you, I hope some of what I share helps you.

I wish you well on your journey. Feedback is always appreciated, you can contact me by e mail paulaosullivan1@gmail.com, and I'll do my best to reply. Or check out my new website www.paulaosullivan. com

May we all feel well,
May we all feel happy, May we all feel loved –

Paula O'Sullivan xxx

Chapter 1

A Story of Creation

There's a story about God. No it wasn't a male or a female, although it contained the elements in equal balance of masculine and feminine. It was an amazing spark of Divine Consciousness. It was perfect, whole and complete. A pulsing expression of unconditional love. And it existed in this perfectness for a long time.

But one day it became aware of itself, and it asked 'What am I?' and 'What am I not?' It knew nothing that wasn't God.

So it decided to create parts of itself so that it would know what it was.

So this God created the universes, the skies and the stars, the planets and galaxies. It created the earth, and the oceans. The plants and the trees, flowers, insects and mammals. And it enjoyed very much experiencing these new aspects of its awareness.

But something was missing. So this God created humans and other beings.

All of the creations recognized the God within themselves and each other, and there was harmony and peace. But after a while some of Gods creations got bored knowing that they were a part of God, they wanted to know what 'was not' God.

God had given these creations free will, and they freely chose to forget their Divine beginnings. So there was day and night, there was light and dark, and there were creations who remembered the God within them, and there were those who forgot over time.

The ones who forgot, lost all remembrance of the God within themselves and others, and with that they lost the awareness of love. They were now alone, separate and disconnected. They spent eternities searching futilely for something outside of themselves that would make them feel complete.

But the veil of illusion was thick. The amnesia remained. And no one remembered that from God they all came and to God eventually they'd return. They were named 'the fallen ones.'

Wars and atrocities began as the disconnected sought to destroy all that wasn't the same in colour, creed or status. This would only end one way.

It was thought wise by some of Gods guardians, the aware ones, to contain this lack of remembrance to one planet called Earth, in case this contagion spread out into the galaxies and infected other civilizations with unawareness. So an etheric web was placed around the planet.

Earth became a hell of sorts where souls incarnated to try to accelerate their awareness. To be in the world but not of it became a very real challenge. Those who incarnated with a semblance of the light within, the kind people with hearts of gold, soon became disillusioned, depressed, anxious, addicted or suicidal. It wasn't easy to live in a world that had forgotten its divineness.

We are the fallen ones, if only we could just remember who we really are.

PAULA O'SULLIVAN
What's it All About?

So why are we so fecking miserable anyway?

Are you suffering from the 'same shit, different day' scenario in your life? Is your life a collection of experiences, that when you look back and observe, you can see a pattern emerging?

You leave a job, because you aren't being treated right, or you're being bullied, or not paid enough. You find a new job, and the same shit happens again. Then you leave and find another job, and the same shit happens again. You get fed up leaving jobs, so you decide to stay. But you can't cope with this as it makes you feel powerless, so you begin to feel ill regularly, or you get depressed, or you have accidents, or you begin to drink more alcohol or eat in excess, or you do whatever you feel you need to do in order to help you cope.

But it's not working, because the pain you feel inside is still there, and you still have to go into that job, so that you can pay your bills. Hell isn't it? A question for any of you who have experienced this, was it the job or was it the people that was your reason for leaving?

Perhaps you look back at your relationships, and they all blur into different faces but the same situations, over and over and over, and you wonder what the heck is going on? How did you get into this again? You left the last relationship thinking you'd do better next time round, but here you are with a lingering feeling of Déjà vu.

Or perhaps you never manage to find a person to have a deeply satisfying relationship with. Maybe the people you keep attracting are all emotionally unavailable or abusers of some kind? Maybe your friends or family take you for granted or treat you badly? What's that all about?

3

You may well begin to wonder at the absurdity of it all. You may keep asking yourself 'Why was I born? What is my purpose? What is the meaning of life? Why the feck am I here?'

If we are to begin breaking the patterns, we need first to understand a little bit about where those patterns came from. Every effect has a cause and every cause has an effect. Yes, some patterns are created in our early childhood years, some are created by our ancestors and get passed down energetically from generation to generation, through our families and though our emotional conditioning. There are social patterns we conform to also, and then there are other energetic patterns that travel with us from our past lives, which we have no conscious awareness of as these patterns are buried deep in our subconscious minds, which can resurface suddenly and create misery for us.

But before I go into all that I'd like to share some of my background experiences. This knowledge I share was hard earned. Some of it you may recognize from your own journey, some of what I say may be wayyyy out there. I'm not asking anyone to agree with me, I'm not trying to prove anyone or anything wrong. Some things have worked for me, and some things haven't. I'm sharing what has worked. Believe what you like, as long as you are happy, content and at peace, that's all that matters. Of course you don't have to read all of this, you can jump straight into the section on Thoughts. I won't be offended, I promise!

Growing up

First I'd like to say, I have an amazing family. I have two sisters and a niece who is only four years younger than me, so she's like a sister to me. They're the best, most kind-hearted people I've ever met, and I am blessed that we are family. I had a dad, a mum and a brother but they have all passed on.

I just want to show you an idea of what it felt like for me growing up, then I can build on that and show you how I coped and overcame the issues that resulted from my early experiences. On this journey I'm on, I've now embraced the philosophy that we're here on earth to experience different things, to teach and to learn. But I didn't know this early on, so like most people I suffered from my life experiences, I didn't know how to seek the lessons and hidden messages in all that happened. And over the years I adopted a victim mentality.

We can't have great relationships with anyone unless we have a great relationship with ourselves first. However we learn how to have relationships from our parents, siblings and peers when we are growing up. If they don't have a great relationship with themselves, which unfortunately was the way with my parents' generation, and possibly is still this way for most of us, then we might experience a bit of dysfunction.

I think I came from the Pleiades, I've certainly felt like an alien for most of my life. Why were people so complicated? How come they just couldn't say what they mean or mean what they say? Why all the lies, the games and cover ups? Why did the people who told you that they loved you not match their words with their actions? Why did the people in my life not tell each other what they really wanted or expected, why did they expect everyone to second guess or mind read? Why did it seem necessary to continue pretending to be someone or something you're not, so that those nearest and dearest would accept this version of you instead of the real you? None of it made any sense.

Not everyone's childhood is all good or all bad. We forget sometimes exactly what people say, but we rarely forget how it makes us feel. The strong emotions that are evoked in us we remember.

These seep deep into our subconscious minds and become a silent background programme which can influence our lives until we can re-programme it. Deep, deep, work as I discovered.

My parents had a lot going on when I arrived fourteen years after my older sister. They had just set up a new business, my older brother had been just diagnosed with mental illness. Then my younger sister appeared a year after me. Utter chaos for them. In their defense they weren't given a manual for parenting, they were just reinforcing the patterns that they were taught. They were doing the best they knew how, based on the imprints they'd received on how to raise kids. Same as most parents.

I just always felt like I wasn't wanted. I really thought there must be something wrong with me. It was only when I started doing personal development work on myself that I began to understand, but even at that it's like layers, you feel you have it sorted, then find out it's deeper than you thought. My latest discovery is The Emotion Code by Dr Bradley Nelson, and yes I will be referring to this throughout this book. When I started releasing emotions, oh boy, then I fully understood what my parents were going through. It's like a life review, but I'll tell you all about that further on.

I don't have too many memories from my early years, but I do have a few from when I was five. I remember asking God to allow me to die in my sleep and being disappointed when I woke up the next day. I was mentally old at that age. I remember my first day at school, all the other children ran to the corner of the room where there was lots of toys to play with. I stood watching them somberly, feeling like I was too old for that kind of stuff. My early photos show a pale unhappy looking girl with a vacant look in her eyes. The lights are on, but nobody's home!

I always felt disconnected, distant and uneasy around people as I was growing up. Looking back, there was an unspoken sense of despair, hopelessness and depression within my family and none of us seemed very close in those years. For me there was a lack of meaningful communication and a sense of numbness and detachment.

My brother was 16 years older than me and was suffering from severe schizophrenia and wasn't always on medication. Even when he was on it, it was still very upsetting. On two occasions the house nearly caught fire as he was careless with his cigarette butts. I could overhear him arguing frequently with the devil and other demons. I never did find out who won that. He was my minder a lot of the time as my Mother was working.

He told me of many things to be afraid of. There wasn't just something waiting under my bed, there were things that came down the chimney, and things that waited on the hall landing for me if I needed to go to the bathroom at night. I was afraid then to leave the bed at night, so that caused its own issues. It took me a long time to free myself of the fear and terror that was instilled in me. And yet he was kind and generous when he could be. It was confusing for a young child.

There were frequent arguments with my father and my siblings. If my younger sister and I made noise in the house while my father was in his room, we would be hit viciously with his belt. I don't know how long this went on for. Luckily this didn't continue. My mother was busy, mostly detached but cheerful at times, she was very passive. There were no hugs, no emotion. My mother suffered with Acrophobia, so didn't like going out much. My parents were self-employed, busy and unavailable emotionally, but at least they provided for us materially, they had money.

I couldn't seem to gain their love and approval in a way that I needed, I couldn't figure it out. I remember one time when I was about

11, I made a decision to eat lots and lots of food. My mother and older sister had some excess weight on, and they seemed to be close, so I thought if I was like them, they would be close to me. By the time my confirmation came around (a religious ceremony from the Catholic tradition) I couldn't get a suit to fit me in the regular shops, so one had to be made for me, it was rather unflattering. I soon realized that eating more food wasn't going to get the results I wanted, and it was just making me feel even uglier than ever. So my weight balanced out again after a while.

So I grew up feeling unloved, worthless, unseen, unheard, depressed, stupid, anxious and ugly. I'm not saying that those nearest and dearest didn't love me, just maybe that they didn't know how to show me their feelings in a way that was meaningful for me. I was sharing my experiences with someone a few years ago and they say said to me, that they had worse experiences than me. It's not a competition folks, we are all allowed validation for how we feel. Not everyone will 'get' or understand you. Not feeling loved bothers some people, and others are immune to it. It bothered me.

According to author Gary Chapman in his book 'The Five Love Languages' there are five ways to experience and express love. Physical touch, words of affirmation, quality time, receiving or giving gifts, and acts of service - examples of devotion. My parents expressed themselves through gifts. I'm kinesthetic so need physical touch the most, but would also feel loved with genuine words, actions and quality time.

These things require the expenditure of great energy levels, most people have barely enough energy to just get out of bed and function on auto pilot for the day. They don't know how to maintain their own energy levels enough to be able to give this kind of energy to others (I share how to do this in the section on energy) so gifts are the easier option. My busy parents did the best they could. I know I sound ungrateful, but it took me a long time to really appreciate gifts as an expression of love. I just wanted to feel loved, and love to me was connection and hugs. I have never been the materialistic type. I really appreciate gifts now but it took me a while to get here.

When I found out only recently about the five love languages, I laughed to myself. How much I suffered all my life so far thinking I wasn't loved, and maybe that wasn't the case after all, or was it? Having said that I also realized that this set up my template for future relationships. I learned from this early conditioning to stay in abusive relationships even when the words didn't match the actions. I also realized that society has us all conditioned to believe conditional love is normal. Stay quiet and I love and reward you... maybe. But make noise and the belt comes out in force. Is that really love? Or is it someone who has no other outlet for their frustration?

My father mostly discouraged me, he transferred his own fears onto me. One time when I was in my teens, I asked if I could help him with his business. He brought me along and then introduced me as his daughter, but told them not to pay any mind to me as I was only a waster. I was mortified, upset and angry. He had a way of making disparaging comments in a joking kind of way. I always felt there was a truth underneath the jokes. I would suggest ways to build his business or share ideas I had for starting something up myself, but he would tell me, that it had been lucky for him to do it, but that I would fail, that it wouldn't work for me. This became my inner mantra. I will fail. I'm a waster. I'm no good. I can't. It took me a long time to override this. As I think back on this I'm detached and I'm laughing because it wasn't personal, in hindsight he called us all gobshites and wasters.

He wasn't all bad. If I needed a loan or a lift though he would help me out, and in later years we did have some fun times arranging poetry supper nights. Looking back I can understand that he had a hard upbringing. His mum died when he was only 11 and his dad bailed out on them and went to England, they were taken in by neighbours.

My mum was so very detached with me, I guess that was her way of surviving. She was very generous though and was always buying little gifts for us. She was cheerful despite all the things she had to deal with, and she had so much to deal with. I so wanted so much to be close to her. I guess most of my life from childhood I was always looking for a pal, someone to connect with on a deep level and be able to communicate openly with.

Ok as a child I couldn't do anything about the fact that I wasn't feeling loved, I was stuck there until I decided to leave when I was 21. But these early experiences created a conditioning in me, as I felt I wasn't being seen, heard or openly encouraged, celebrated or appreciated, in a way that I needed, I developed very low self- esteem. No one to blame, it's just the way I perceived my reality. Ha, isn't hindsight a wonderful thing!

Strangely enough though, as I grew up and started working, the people I met seemed to see something in me that made them want to destroy or crush me even further, which helped me to feel even more wrong and wretched. It took me a long time before I discovered why that was and what I could do about it, I'll share about this in the section on self-esteem.

Right up until my mid-forties I couldn't think for myself and looked to others to make the decisions for me. I just felt so wrong, that I didn't trust myself to know what was best for me. I gave my power away.

Being an Empath

Someone said to me recently that people are not born as an empath, but their experiences create that. I think I agree with them in a way. I also think some of us come into this world a tad more sensitive than others. An empath is someone who can read between the lines, they know if you're lying deep down. They know if you're not being authentic. They can be sensitive to energy changes.

Some can feel people's real emotions and pain. If they don't know about this they can take on others emotions and pain and believe it belongs to them. In fact I believe that most of us are like sponges absorbing other people's emotional crap! Empaths sometimes know if people are sending negative thoughts and emotions to them, and sometimes that can make them ill. I'll share more about this in a section about psychic attack. Empaths can be highly intuitive.

I didn't know I was an empath until I was in my forties, but looking back, at some stage I became one in my childhood. I couldn't make sense of my world. It all just seemed so pointless. People were saying one thing but doing something else. I struggled to gain the approval of my parents, but nothing seemed to be enough, I just didn't feel wanted.

Even in my early stages of adulthood I never could find the elusive 'proper job'. I tried not to rock the boat by having different opinions, I tried to fit in, but I never felt accepted, in fact I still don't fully feel accepted by my world and I still haven't found a proper job! It's ok though, I accept myself now and that's all that matters. It's just the way the world is. You can't expect people to love and accept you when most people don't even love and accept themselves. Knowing this makes it a little easier to cope with.

Over the years there were times when I got too close to unearthing peoples bullshit when they were not being honest with me, and they tried to label me crazy, or told me I had a great imagination, or that I was very sensitive, as if that was a crime. I laughed when I read somewhere that nothing upsets narcissists more than being accused of something they actually did! But in the deepest wisest core of myself I had an inner knowing which I held fast to, even if in some way I had begun believing that maybe I was going to end up like my brother who was mentally ill.

However I received validation some years later from one of those people, who asked me how the feck did I know the truth, and that it had scared the crap out of them! And over time other things were validated for me, so I learned to trust myself more. I still use discernment though as every situation has to be evaluated differently.

Empaths become people pleasers. They are always the ones in relationships who try to understand. They try to anticipate everyone else's needs. They are the ones who keep giving people extra chances. They are the ones who do everything to prove their innocence. They do everything to make sure that they aren't misunderstood. And they carry oh way too much guilt, because they have created a template of perfection which they measure themselves against.

They won't leave a person or situation until they have tried everything they can think of to make it work. They always try to understand how it is from the others perspective, and for some crazy reason they choose to root for the other person first, even over themselves.

We are all just beautiful people who just want to love and be loved, we give and give and give, and don't feel worthy enough to receive. And if by some accident we do receive something, then the guilt trip begins again, about there being someone more deserving than us.

Many empaths stay in abusive, dysfunctional relationships and situations, hoping things will change, which they rarely do, because
both the abuser and the abused need to reinforce each other. No
I'm not talking about situations with kids here, and no this isn't an
excuse for anyone to abuse, if a person is destroying someone, they
have issues, not the person who is being abused. Well we all have
issues of a kind. But if the person who is being abused suddenly re-
alizes their inner worth, do you think they will tolerate staying with
an abuser for much longer? Well hell no.

You will only allow people to treat you in a way that you somehow
feel deep down inside that you deserve, nothing more and nothing
less. And yes it's complicated. There were times when I realized my
worth but was unable to leave situations or people who were harming me, due to my need to feel approved of, to not feel guilty, to not
be a quitter, to have some basic needs met of not being alone.

I deal with this is a section about meeting your un-met needs. From
where I am at right now after all the work I've done on myself over
the years, I have reached zero tolerance level for anyone who shows
me disrespect. I'm beginning to really love the sound of my feet
walking away from anything or anyone that harms me!

It's possible to remain an empath and to learn what is yours and what
is theirs, you can separate your energy, your emotions, your thoughts
and feelings. It's possible to learn healthy boundaries and become
assertive instead of aggressive, and it's possible to love yourself and
equally include yourself when needs are being met without the guilt
trip. These are some of the kind of things I've accomplished and that
I'll share in this book.

Depression

I fell into the abyss, probably from the age of five. But I didn't even know that I was in there, it all just seemed normal to me, living in misery, day after day after day. I've been in and out of the abyss more than a few times in my life, and I've never once sent a postcard with 'Wish you were here' on it! It's not a good place to be!

I found out that you can't leave the abyss until you've actually acknowledged that you are in one to begin with! You can't change anything until you bring awareness of your current reality to mind. I was just so depressed, but I couldn't talk about it to anyone. I was so afraid I'd end up like my brother.

Oh I know many people say that depression is a chemical imbalance and that we are all victims of our highly intelligent systems, but I think otherwise. From research I've done since over the years, I came to the conclusion that chemical imbalances don't just appear randomly, they are caused by something.

Maybe you've spent your whole life surrounded by assholes? Perhaps you were unloved, abused, bullied? Were brought up in an environment of depressed people and you entrained to depressive tendencies? Maybe you were a magnet for Narcissists? You had a poor diet? Grew up in poverty? Believed what they told you about Fluoridated water and drank loads of it? All these things and more can change the chemicals in your body.

When you are stressed the body secretes excess chemicals of cortisol and adrenalin into your system to help you to cope. The body stops over producing them when you become calmer. If you don't become calmer, if the things that are stressing you are in your face all the time then the body keeps producing and producing. The chemical imbalances are a result rather than the cause I believe.

I felt depressed most of my life until about 2010, when I learned some techniques that helped raise my awareness, that's when the healing really began. I never did try medication, I didn't see it curing anyone close to me, and so I didn't trust it. Just to mention here, everybody is different and sometimes it is necessary though, so don't feel bad if you did have to go on it. Some people have told me that the medications numb you from feeling things too deeply, that it can feel like there is cotton wool between you and your reality, maybe it can help people cope.

There aren't many people around giving alternative solutions, so I personally understand how painful it can be trying to deal with it if you suffer with depression. Always consult your doctor and don't go rushing off to drop your medications after reading this, which can be dangerous. Stuff builds up in your system and takes time to leave it, which should be done slowly and under supervision. I've seen a few people crash and burn after ditching their meds, and it's not a pretty sight, they were always worse off than before, don't do it!

After a while practicing techniques, I summed up the depression I was experiencing as this: 'I was feeling depressed because of my inability to accept my current reality and I felt powerless to be able to change it.' That then led me into exploring some of my core beliefs, which I'll share later.

No I'm not saying it can be cured. There will always be assholes out there that'll trigger you… just kidding. I'll share how to stop attracting assholes later! Yes there are things outside of your control that can contribute to feelings of depression, but that's not the complete story. Everything has a cause and an effect. Feelings of depression or anything else for that matter are the effects of something. It's your thoughts about those people or situations that lead you to feel depressed. You are not the victim of circumstances that you've been told you are.

Let me remind you of my statement regarding the depression I experienced. I felt unable to change anything and I couldn't accept the situations I was in. Now where can you go with something like that? Around and around in a circle spiraling rapidly downwards at best me thinks.

Ok so the people you're surrounded by and how they treat you will either make you feel good or bad to a certain extent, and if you continue to hang out with them, they will affect you, as will the environment you're in. It's called entrainment or resonance. I'll explain about that later on. The food you eat, the water you drink will change how chemicals will be released in your body. But most importantly it's the thoughts you think about anyone or anything that creates the feeling you will feel in any given situation that will signal to the brain to release or suppress what the body feels it needs most to help you to survive at all costs.

If you find yourself in a situation where you can't change it, accept it or run away from it either mentally or physically. The only way your body can help you is to place you in a state of depression or illness. The state of depression is your safety valve. It shuts you off to stimuli that you can't deal with. You will then be able to avoid situations and people in a way. No it's not perfect, but if you understand how the body and mind work, you will see that it is trying to protect you always. The problem is, it becomes an automatic response to everything you can't see yourself dealing with, so you remain depressed or ill and feeling really bad… which is not good.

Also notice that I called it the depression, rather than my depression. I learnt how to not identify with it. As long as it was my depression, I was attached to it. That attachment was feeding some need in me. It was serving some positive purpose, otherwise I couldn't have continued to be depressed. Now maybe you're wondering what on earth could be a positive purpose behind being depressed! Well at the time I didn't know about energy and how we use it. Someone wrote somewhere that depression could be interpreted as a need for deep rest. And anyone who has suffered, knows how little energy you have when you are in that state of mind.

So you sleep a lot, which gives the body a chance to rest and do repairs. At the time I was anxious and fearful, I had low self- esteem and very little confidence. Having to engage socially was exhausting, it was better to have depression which helped me to avoid people and situations that I was unable to cope with, because back then I didn't know how to change things, and I didn't have the energy to try.

Another positive intention of depression for me was it was like an 'opt- out' clause for trying new things. My sense of worth was nil, I didn't feel I could do things, so it took the pressure off me, in a way. To be honest after all the work I've done, I think you could be trying to cure depression all your life and not really get anywhere. But if you first deal with any self- esteem issues, there's a very good chance that you'll get somewhere, and like me, you may even overcome the tendency to be depressed most of the time.

I read a book about 'Choice Theory' by William Glasser. It was very interesting, and I'm sure he pissed a lot of people off by suggesting that we choose to be depressed among other things! However as I read and practiced some of his theories, I did arrive at a place where I broke free. I did realize that I had a choice. As I practiced other techniques, which I'll share as much of as I can in this book to help you, I learned how to change my thoughts, which changed how I felt, which led me out of my auto response state of depression. I

17

also learned how to energetically release trapped emotions that were causing a resonance within me that was attracting people and situations that exacerbated feelings of depression, feeling unworthy and so on. I'll share more about that later.

And then came the day when I no longer waited for each day to see how I felt emotionally. I would decide each evening that tomorrow, if I woke up, it would be a good day. I stopped berating myself for my unforgivable lack of perfection, I reminded myself that I was doing the best I can, and when I could do better, I would do better. If I fucked up that day, even though it made me feel bad, I would pledge to try to be more aware next time and improve myself and my interactions.

I stopped dreading the next day and began to look forward to it, and I started to observe myself rather than judge. When I woke up I would decide that I would do the best I could to enjoy the day. I would focus on the many different things I was grateful for. I was able to choose different thoughts, which over time became my default way of thinking, which insured that I was feeling good most of the time. Relief!

Now I won't lie to you, I'm not perfect, I'm human. I've had to deal with some really heavy shit over the years. There are occasional days when I do get overwhelmed. So I rest, meditate, and withdraw my energies. I'm an empath so I do need to withdraw now and again and not 'do people'. Occasionally I'll allow myself some wallow in misery time, or a part of a duvet day, but I restrict it. When the allocated time is up, I say 'enough, now what small thing can I do to lift my mood?' 'Shall I read a book, go for a walk, watch a movie, or take some photographs, write or paint?' 'What am I grateful for?' I can always look around me and see what I do have, and off I go again.

Sometimes I'll listen to Solfeggio Frequencies, Brainwave Entrainment music or some Hypnosis for relaxation. I usually check if I have any trapped emotions to release, frequently I absorb stuff from other people which makes me feel crap. And sometimes I just need to sleep, or switch off in order to reboot. Someone quite wittily said that 'Sleep was death without the commitment', it sure is.

Religion

I was raised a Catholic. I was fed the story of the baby Jesus, a son of God who later went on to die for our sins. So why did I grow up still feeling like a sinner? His father, God, was a bit of a meanie sometimes. If you didn't do what pleased him, woe betide you, run and hide because he would seek revenge and have his day! Hence I learned about conditional love and a religious paranoia about being watched all the time. Worse than Santa Claus at Christmas checking if you're being naughty or nice!

That wasn't bad enough for a small child to learn, worse than that I was born a female. Immediate entrance into the level of second class citizen. According to the Bible story of Adam and Eve. Not content to be in paradise, Eve is in the garden and meets a snake who offers her an apple. Didn't anyone warn her not to talk to strangers? So she eats the apple and gives some to her other half, and hey presto, they get fecked out of the garden, because they now know the difference between good and evil, and they are now on an equal par with God? The big sin was to dare think you are equal to God you lowly human. And of course everyone blames Eve for trying to tempt Adam, or so they say.

I never questioned the validity of these stories, I just believed we weren't good enough, God was an external entity far superior to us, and women were to blame for the downfall of mankind, so they were persecuted over the ages, and still are to some extent.

I went to a convent school until I was 11. When I was 7 years old I was being prepared to make my Holy Communion, which has little girls dressed up in white dresses like little brides. We had a thing called confession where you went into a small dark cubicle and sitting behind a grid, a priest waited to hear all your sins. Before I went in I asked a nun what were sins, and she said lying to your parents, stealing and so on. I told her I hadn't done any of those things. She told me to make something up! You couldn't just forgive yourself, a priest had to do that, they knew God better and they were men after all.

I began to see a lot of hypocrisy. I knew someone whose siblings were being abused by a religious brother in a nearby boy's school, and the same religious brother tried to molest me when I was 15, when I was sitting in the schools bike shed one afternoon after school with my first boyfriend. I also saw that contraception wasn't permitted, but if a young girl got pregnant then she was treated like a prostitute, and in a lot of cases forced to leave home.

I eventually stopped believing in a God or higher power. I drank heavily, I was a bit lost for a few years.

When I was in my late 20's I met someone who appeared to be deeply religious and was a protestant with tattoos. It was a turning point. I had just begun socializing with people who were into heavy drugs, and I could see there was a fork in the road and I could so easily have got involved and escaped my pain with one road, but it was perhaps the lure of possible salvation that made me choose the other path.

I got married and I became an avid protestant, I became smug and judgmental thinking that we at least were saved! Gosh if only I had known what I think I know now I wouldn't have been so pompous!

In my mind I was still a lowly worm not equal to God and I was still a woman, but at least I didn't have to confess made up sins. If I wanted to become a minister I knew I could. I enjoyed the social aspects. I enjoyed the direct line to God if I chose to converse with him. We met some really lovely people in the different churches we went to over those years.

It was only after I had left my marriage, and was seeking to explore my spirituality, that I began reading about the Eastern concepts of God, I really liked the Buddhist concepts and others. I changed my beliefs and stopped going to church. It just didn't fit who I was becoming.

Now don't misunderstand me, I'm not saying that those religions are wrong, it is just they were wrong for me. I just needed something more inclusive.

I came across this quote and it took me a while to understand it 'Religion is for people who are afraid of going to hell. Spirituality is for those who have already been there.' – Vine Deloria, Sioux.

I had been in hell most of my life, Spirituality was exactly what I needed. I've been exploring it ever since!

Now that you know a bit about my experiences, I'd like to begin sharing a bit more about where the patterns that cause us pain and separation possibly come from

Why Are Women Treated Like Lesser Beings?

No this isn't a rant about men, if you read to the very end you'll understand that.

I've been asking that question for a long time now. After reading a lot I came across some interesting stories. Maybe this is a bit outrageous, but I'll share a bit of it, make up your own mind. However outrageous you may think this story is, I can tell you it isn't half as outrageous as the way women have been treated over the centuries.

According to some sources there are two Gods mentioned in the Bible. One is a loving God, and that supposedly refers to the Divine Spark. The other God or Gods are called the Creator Gods, sons of God. They are the vengeful God.

They are mentioned in the bible Genesis 6:4 it reads as follows: 'The Nephilim were in the earth in those days, and also after that, when the sons of God came in unto the daughters of men, and they bore children to them; the same were the mighty men that were of old, the men of renown.'

From some sources I read, supposedly there was a mating of Nephilim and human species in ancient times. These were giants so the mating didn't create children because the women weren't able to accommodate the size of the babies. I'm presuming it wasn't an actual physical mating. So further attempts were made. These ancient beings were far advanced in many ways including genetic manipulation. They were of the fallen who wanted to own and control humans. Remains of giants are still being excavated around the world, so apparently they did exist at one time in the past. According to the stories, they then created automatons or things, beings who couldn't think for themselves, perfect slaves. But the women (Eves) still carried a small amount of higher consciousness and a few realized what was happening, and they tried to tell the men (Adams) Adam and Eve represent a generic race rather than just two people. The Eves managed to succeed in awakening the consciousness of a small amount of the Adams (the serpent means wisdom, the apple consciousness, the garden of Eden, is the paradise of the creator Gods with all their slaves)

22

And apparently this my friends, really pissed off the creator Gods.

It's an interesting story isn't it? No less interesting than the one that is so widely accepted and drummed into us from childhood and throughout our lives. So yes women are to blame for caring so much about their fellow men and women to risk trying to waken them up. For ruining their plans, the creator Gods created a patriarchal system which over time persecuted women who showed any signs of having esoteric knowledge or anything that might awaken the consciousness of others. This led to intuition, spiritual awareness, and psychic abilities and so on being treated with suspicion, persecution and death. It was mostly women but some awakened men had to be careful too.

Men were not exactly free of the wrath of the Creator Gods either. To prevent them from being susceptible to being awakened, they were subsequently conditioned over the years to not listen to women. I still see many examples of this today. They were conditioned to not be emotional (emotions link with the feminine energies). They were encouraged to view women as opponents not team players. They were educated to disregard anything that they couldn't see in the physical realms, and even the school systems and psychology were based on this by encouraging left brain analytical learning and evaluation. With very little emphasis if any on right brain creativity or the use of imagination or intuition.

They weren't going to escape being slaves either, the threat in the Bible doesn't come from God, but from the creator Gods. Men would have to work to survive. Women would suffer. And Wisdom (the serpent) would be crushed and disregarded. Well that's my understanding of it.

Let's re read this quote from the Bible, Genesis 13 'Then the LORD God said to the woman, "What is this you have done?" The woman said, "The serpent deceived me, and I ate." 14 So the LORD God said to the serpent, "Because you have done this, "Cursed are you above all livestock and all wild animals! You will crawl on your belly and you will eat dust all the days of your life. 15 And I will put enmity between you and the woman, and between your offspring and hers; he will crush your head, and you will strike his heel." 16 To the woman he said, "I will make your pains in childbearing very severe; with painful labor you will give birth to children. Your desire will be for your husband, and he will rule over you." 17 To Adam he said, "Because you listened to your wife and ate fruit from the tree about which I commanded you, "You must not eat from it," "Cursed is the ground because of you; through painful toil you will eat food from it all the days of your life. 18 It will produce thorns and thistles for you, and you will eat the plants of the field. 19 By the sweat of your brow you will eat your food until you return to the ground, since from it you were taken; for dust you are and to dust you will return."

Is it any wonder the world is the way it is, with men and women conditioned to be so mistrustful of each other and of higher wisdom?

Unfortunately peoples' interpretation of the bible texts which were written by men (not God) approximately 500 years after the first original ones, have caused pain and separation between men and women, between straight and gay people, between people of differing beliefs and skin colour. This is a part of most people's early education and conditioning. It does not encourage the belief that we are good enough, or that we are all connected, or that the Divine spark of God is in us all, and that if we harm one thing, we cause harm to ourselves, energetically.

If a man mates with or rapes a woman and she gets pregnant, the shame is on her supposedly. We've regressed so much from the ancient teachings of Sacred Sexuality, where a woman's womb (the Holy Grail) was revered as a vessel for life. We don't have to look too far to see all the shame that has been placed on women who had children out of marriage. Nobody is interested in the fucker that made them pregnant though, it's obviously the woman's fault. NOT! Where does this concept come from that women are guilty but not the men? And why are people still entertaining it? Well some of it comes from the stories I mentioned about Adam & Eve. Drum that into a lot of innocent little minds of children, pass it on and reinforce it over the generations and this is what happens in my opinion.

But there was more in the bible that encouraged the Patriarchal dominance to continue. The Mary Magdalene story. We're told that Mary was a prostitute, a whore, a sinner but that Jesus is kind to her. In Ireland the Magdalene Laundries, or also known as Magdalene asylums, were run by Roman Catholic nuns and were in operation from the 18th to the late 20th centuries.

Seemingly to house 'fallen women', approximately 30, 000 women were kept in these institutions around Ireland. They were used like slave labour, and their babies given or sold for adoption. Many bodies were found in later years on the grounds of some of these places, of women and babies for which no death cert was registered. What did these women do to deserve this? Nothing, they were the victims of a sick form of social conditioning.

In 325 AD The Council of Nicaea, rearranged and omitted some texts from the bible, and I think it was interfered with more than a few times after that for political reasons. This is where the story of Mary Magdalene being a whore was perpetrated. I found in other places that Mary was described as a priestess and a disciple of equal standing with Jesus. Apparently she became his wife, and the wedding of Cana was their wedding.

Have a read of the book 'Secrets of the Code – The unauthorized guide to the mysteries behind The Da Vinci Code' edited by Dan

Burstein, it's a fascinating collection of articles, well worth a read.

In those times there were priests and priestesses who practiced Sacred Sexuality and provided initiations for males and females at puberty. They taught people how to celebrate the Divine Masculine and the Divine Feminine in each person. They taught them how to have balanced relationships.

Males and females were treated equally and uniquely, but by also acknowledging their strengths and weaknesses they reached a sacred balance. When the new system was put into place, the Patriarchal system (probably led by the Arians) some of these priestesses were forced into prostitution. They were made to stay at their temples and couldn't leave until they had had sex with a man. From what I read Mary Magdalene was not one of those unlucky women, she and her priestesses managed to escape to another area.

Why do I mention all of this? Well it obvious to me anyway after doing a bit of research, that these kinds of things affect our conditioning of how we view ourselves and others, this sort of pain and shame and guilt gets passed down the lines energetically, we all inherit it. If you believe in past lives, we have all been male and females over many, many, past lives. This create patterns that make us suffer in this life time. A cruel trick has been played on all males and females. It's time we reunited once again.

Check out Michael Tsarion's videos or book called 'Atlantis, Alien Visitation & Genetic Manipulation' or 'Edgar Cayce on Atlantis' by Edgar Evans Cayce or do a google search for more about these other subjects.

Reincarnation

For most of my life I didn't know much about the subject of past lives, except the usual jokes you hear about coming back as a chicken or other things. The religions I'd experienced only gave you one life to get it right or you're going straight to hell boyo. It wasn't until I was training as a Hypnotherapist that I learned about the concept of reincarnation.

We did a past life regression one afternoon. After the induction I visualized myself standing on a grassy patch of ground on the outskirts of some buildings. When it was suggested that I look down, I was wearing a brown shift, like a monk would wear. I looked into a barrel of water to see my reflection, and looked upon a deformed face. I saw a handsome man with a pretty woman nearby looking at me.

I kept wishing that I was one of them. I was told in my mind that they were called the O'Brien's. I re visited this lifetime in further meditations and found out that I was a Medieval monk in the 1700's from a village called Oldcastle in Co. Meath, Ireland, who was outcast by a group of local women, who didn't like the look of me, and were suspicious of the sacred knowledge that I was trying to share. Can I prove it? No, but I find it's an interesting possibility.

Over the past few years I've experienced quite a few regressions and meditations, and apparently I've had a few life times in priestly roles including the one already mentioned. A Celtic Monk, Tibetan Monk, Knights Templar (twice) and a Nun. In all of them I was trying to share knowledge. I'm still finding out about other lives I've had.

From what I've read about the subject, our souls spiritually agree before we are born, who we are going to be born to, what environment we'll grow up in, and what souls will incarnate in groups. Some change roles over different lifetimes to help each other with their life mission. Some will be a brother in one life time, and then be a father in the next, or a mother, child or friend for example.

If you were against anyone or anything in one lifetime, you might decide on a soul level to incarnate as a person of a certain religion or colour for example. If you were homophobic in one lifetime you may come back as someone who is inclined to be homosexual, or one of your family might, in order for you to understand life from that perspective and learn tolerance.

This makes great sense to me. If you look around your world you will see, separation, segregation, racism and so on. People are divided from each other based on beliefs, colours, creeds etc. that's because we are not aware that we are all one. We have been divided and that's how you conquer and control the masses, set them against themselves.

From a reincarnation perspective, over many lifetimes, you've experienced yourself in many parts as group souls in insects and animals, plants and life forms, as your awareness progressed you've been a man, and a woman, you've been a victim and a persecutor. Some still are. Now most of us forget our previous life times, which is just as well because this lifetime is difficult enough, but it is possible to find out some of them through regression or emotional clearing.

The purpose of this is not for amusement but to regain awareness and raise consciousness. To try to heal unexplained fears, patterns or illnesses. To become a better version of yourself, to love unconditionally and to accept all beings as they are with the level of awareness they have reached.

Apparently from what I've read in a few places we are only experiencing an aspect of our higher soul in this life time, so that all the lessons learnt over all the other past lives are not lost. From my understanding of what I've read, we have a soul and it splits into aspects, like the God story, that we can become aware of what we are, and what we are not, to become aware of our Divinity or lack of it.

Sometimes our soul will create a few aspects that come to earth at the same time. If you meet an aspect of yourself, you find that you become lost in that relationship. It's kinda like meeting a soul mate I think, and it's not always running off into the sunset, when you do meet them. Sometimes it can be very challenging. Check out 'Soul Psychology' by Dr. Joshua Stone for more about this concept. Fascinating.

A few years ago I met a guy at a meditation class and we seemed to have almost identical spiritual knowledge, we knew a lot of similar concepts and it was uncanny. We met up a few times for coffee, and one day went on a day trip to an area I wasn't very familiar with. There was a fork in the paths and one led up a steep incline and the other led downwards at a moderate incline. He was trying to persuade me to take the higher path which led to a cliff edge. But for some reason I couldn't understand I was filled with an inner sense of terror. So I chose the lower path.

When we were having coffee later, we began discussing past lives, when he told me he had been a Tibetan Monk, I felt a shiver and understood my previous unease. As I also had a lifetime as a Tibetan Monk, and apparently I took a dare and jumped off a cliff to my death, with some other monks to prove reincarnation. I wondered if that person beside me was one of those monks, reincarnated! Made me laugh anyway!

I always took for granted that our past lives would be on Earth, but I recently started using The Emotion Code, which I'll share about later, and I found that as I was releasing energetic trapped emotions, some were trapped in this life time, some inherited from my parents and ancestors, and some had travelled with me from life times in other dimensions and planets. Apparently I've spent many life times on and off earth trying to share sacred knowledge, and not meeting with much success. And here I am again, trying to share stuff that most people don't believe in! Is it true? I don't know, but I find it interesting!

The concept of reincarnation or of past lives is based on the belief that our soul is eternal. Many Eastern religions include this belief. It is said that the church fathers altered texts in the Bible at the Council of Nicaea and omitted reincarnation, creating a concept of one life instead of many lives. However some people think that the use of the word resurrection in the Bible actually refers to reincarnation. It was easier to control people with a concept of Heaven and Hell and only one life or one chance to get it right. Fear is a powerful motivator.

There is also the concept of Karma in Eastern religions, which implies that a soul travels through many lifetimes and experiences. It is believed that we were all sparks of the Divine Source (God) or whatever you would like to call it, we got separated from this Divineness, and we got caught up in a reality of duality, fear, sickness and death, we come back again and again, to heal the hurts and pain, to right the wrongs of our actions in the past lives of unawareness, to rise above ego mind, and one day reunite with the Divineness that is both outside and within us.

We reap what we sow, everything has a cause and an effect, and all our actions are noted in the Akashic Records, a book that is held in an etheric Hall of Records. Not for the purpose of judgement but for the raising of consciousness, so that in your life review you get to feel the feelings of all your experiences and how you affected others. What we do to others in Karma will be done to us, whether in the lifetime we do it, or in some future lifetime.

However there is also information I read about forgiveness of ourselves and others which can neutralize Karma. Our past lives can affect how we are today, it can affect health, weight problems, phobias, relationships etc. I have had some people present themselves for Reiki with throat issues, who believed they were beheaded in a past life for example. There were some really barbaric practices in ancient times.

Energy carries consciousness as discovered in Quantum Theory the Observer Effect. We are energetically connected to everything else including our past energetic patterns. We come to learn our life lessons then we get to evolve and move on. The more we develop our consciousness / awareness, the quicker we pay off our Karmic depts. And the less chance we have of creating more Karma. Which means more peaceful future lives, but the heck with that, we'll forget, so that lesson will be lost to us on a conscious level.

For me knowing all this is helping me to create a better life now. I'm learning why some people don't like me, or why I'm uneasy with some. I'm learning that some people appear in my life and try to unconsciously pick up where they left off some couple of thousand years ago. Do I still want to be treated like someone's mistress? Feck no. Yes I've made some mistakes and I've learned from them. Guilt trips are over I'm acting consciously from now on.

Do I still want to be mistreated? No way. Do I want to abuse or mistreat anyone? Not in this lifetime darling. Do I want to be a racist or to be judgmental? What a waste of all those past lives if I did. And this is a biggie, do I ever feel the need to contemplate suicide? No, not anymore, not since I started to research all this, because I know I'll have to just come back and face all the unlearned lessons in some other life, and that maybe just maybe it would be worse than I have now.

I think as some Buddhists do, that you can raise your awareness to a certain point, that it gives you some kind of spiritual choice when you pass over for your next adventure. The object being that you escape the wheel of karma, and stop having to keep reincarnating on earth. Apparently there are many dimensions and levels that can be chosen when consciousness reaches more aware levels.

I like this better than the concepts of heaven and hell. I don't have to wait until I die, I've found both here on earth anyway, many, many times.

If you would like to try a past life regression, I've included one here. Record your voice and put some calm music behind it, audacity is a great program for doing this. Or get a friend to read it out slowly for you. Enjoy!

Past Life Regression Meditation

Sit or lie down and make yourself very comfortable, when you are ready, close your eyes and breathe in slowly and deeply, imagining that your breath is travelling up from the tips of your fingers up your arms to your head, chest and belly on the in breath, and out and down your body, through your legs, feet and toes, on the out breath. Breathing in love and light, breathing out any worries or cares.

Ask for protection from God, Angels, or Spirit Guides etc. 'Thank you for your shield of protection and healing while I undertake this journey. If anything tries to interfere with my mind, body, spirit or consciousness on any level of my being except by your Divine Permission, please return to sender in the form of love and light, so that no harm or karma be created, thank you.'

Imagine that you are in a most beautiful, peaceful sanctuary garden.

You are lying down on the lovely soft green grass, the sky up ahead is the most wonderful vibrant blue, and the sun is shining warmly on your skin, and yes you're wearing sun protection, and yes you feel very safe here. There is a soft gentle warm breeze and you can hear birds twittering away merrily in the nearby trees.

You feel the sun warming your toes on your left foot, and you feel it warming your whole foot, and you feel it warming your ankle... Your left foot feels so warm and relaxed...

You feel the sun warming your toes on your right foot, and you feel it warming your whole foot, and you feel it warming your ankle... Your right foot feels so warm and relaxed...

You feel the sun warming your calf and knee on your left leg and your left leg relaxes...

You feel the sun warming your calf and knee on your right leg and your right leg relaxes...

Now you feel the sun warming your thigh on your left leg... your thigh relaxes on your left leg... you feel your whole left leg relax

Now you feel the sun warming your thigh on your right leg... your thigh relaxes on your right leg... you feel your whole right leg relax

You notice the warmth of the sun on your belly now... All the muscles in your belly respond to the warmth... and they relax...

Your hips feel the warmth of the sun... and they relax

You feel the warmth of the sun on the fingers of your left hand... you feel it warming the back of your left hand ... And you feel it warming your wrist... Your left hand relaxes...

You feel the warmth of the sun on the fingers of your right hand… you feel it warming the back of your right hand… And you feel it warming your wrist… Your right hand relaxes…

The sun warms your left arm all the way up to your left shoulder… your left arm relaxes…

The sun warms your right arm all the way up to your right shoulder… your right arm relaxes…

You feel the sun warm your chest, making you relax even more, you experience a deeply contented relaxed feeling…your chest relaxes…

The sun warms your neck…. Your neck feels very comfortable and relaxed…

You feel the warmth of the sun on your face… Your left cheek feels very relaxed… Now your right cheek feels relaxed… Now your nose feels relaxed… And your forehead feels relaxed… Now your jaw relaxes… And your eyes relax… Now your left ear relaxes… And your right ear relaxes… Now your whole head is relaxed…

You look around the sanctuary and notice an unusual looking building in the corner almost hidden by some bushes with fragrant flowers… there is a gateway and a doorway…

You enter and find yourself in a long corridor with many doors on either side…. You walk up and down past the doors…. One door in particular draws your attention…. This is the doorway to a past life that is most relevant to your present lifetime… this past life will help you to understand what you most need to learn in this lifetime. Before you walk through the door… know that if anything you see or feel or hear affects you in an emotionally upsetting way… all you have to do is float above it and watch it from a third perspective, or any stage you can just open your eyes and be back in your room... think of it like you are watching a movie... you are perfectly safe... When you are ready open the door...

You will remember everything you see... you are here to gather information that is most relevant to your life now... you will find out what you came to learn in this lifetime... you will remember everything that you need to remember... your mind is very powerful and it always serves to protect you... it will allow you to see and remember what you need to know...

Walk through the doorway... into your childhood of a past life ...

Find something that reflects your image in this past life, a mirror or some water... Look and see who you are... a boy or a girl? What age are you? What are your wearing? Are you wearing shoes, sandals, are you barefoot? What colour are your eyes? What colour is your hair? What colour is your skin?

Look around you...Where are you? What country is this? What year? What is your childhood like? What is your home like, is it a house or a dwelling, part of a village, or a tribe, or something else, where do you live? Explore your surroundings, take everything in and remember it.

Who are your parents? Look into their eyes. Do you have siblings? Look into their eyes. Who are the significant people for you in this lifetime? Look into their eyes. Are any of them familiar in your present lifetime? Souls travel through time together to help each other heal and grow. Ask them have they any message for you to bring back to your present life, is there anything you need to pay attention to?

Float out of this childhood now and into a later time in this past life

… were you working? … What did you work at? Who were your employers? How was your experience with them? Look around your place of employment? Remember everything.

What else happen in this past life? Did you get married? Did you have children? What were those relationships like?

Float out of this part of your past life and into a part where something major happened to you in this past life? What happened? How did you feel? How did it affect you and the way you thought and acted?

If anything is too upsetting, detach yourself and float above it and watch it like a movie playing out…. is there any connection with this experience in your past life and your experiences or actions in this present lifetime?

Float above this past life experience and onto anything else that happened in this past life that you need to be aware of…..

Now float into the time of your death… if anything is too upsetting, detach yourself and float above it… where are you? Take a note of your surroundings and remember. What happened? How did you die? Were you alone or with people? Were there friends or family with you? Did you have a life review? What did you learn from that lifetime?

Now it is time to leave this past life and return to your present lifetime, you will remember everything that you need to remember… make your way back towards the door that you entered… back through the gateway and into the garden sanctuary…. The warm sun is still shining brightly, the birds are still twittering away merrily…as you leave the garden sanctuary …

You feel the sensations of aliveness in your toes and feet and legs and arms… wriggle your toes… wriggle your fingers and move your arms and legs… become aware again of your breathing….each breath energizes you… become aware of your surroundings… and now bring yourself gently back into the room… remembering everything you need to remember. Namaste in love and light.

What You Need to Know Before You Can Change Something

Resistance

Have you ever tried to change anything in your life but found that it is really difficult to do it? You may start off great, you lose a few pounds in weight, then bam, you're back into your old habits again and it's worse than before. Or you try to leave a job or a relationship and after a few feeble attempts you resign yourself to being stuck where you are, in fact it's kind of like the saying, 'The Devil you know is better than the Devil you don't know', and you settle yourself back into the uncomfortable familiar situations again and again. Feeling even more of a failure than you did before.

Why is it that you seem to only be able to take two steps forward and then it seems like you have to take six steps back. It's like the fecking cha- cha except the moves are wrong.

Well as I mentioned, and will keep mentioning, some of this is about energy. I'll share more about 'entrainment' later, but for now, you should know that all living creatures harmonize energetically for the purpose of conserving energy. You will entrain to the most dominant energy because it's easier.

What could be a dominant energy? Well this could be thoughts, core beliefs, expectations or emotions, it could also be the interactions of cells in our body and brain. We become used to thinking and feeling a certain way. Our thoughts create our feelings. Our body then gets used to those patterns. We form neural pathways in the brain the more we think certain thoughts, these then become our automatic way of thinking (entrainment again) our bodies also produce different chemicals depending on the thoughts and emotions we have regularly.

In researching this I came across Candace Pert Ph.D. who describes the release of neuropeptides throughout the body whenever we feel a certain emotion, our cells then build receptors to accommodate them. Our bodies get used to receiving those neuropeptides, and when we try to change a way we have been thinking or feeling when challenged with a situation which would have previously have received a negative response for example if you're trying to think positive, or if you're trying to quit something, we may get resistance. You cells will want the usual chemicals. It's very like an addiction and going cold turkey when you try to give it up.

In order to change anything we have to change the underlying programs that are running quietly in the background. This requires large amounts of energy at the beginning. Then it becomes somewhat easier.

Your thoughts are so important, much more than you know. Everything gets created with your thoughts. When you change your thoughts, you create new neural pathways. Repetition is so important. If you went to school how did you learn? By repeating stuff over and over and over again until it stuck in your mind. Well this kind of personal development work is the same. As you change how you think, you will change how you feel. When you change how you feel, you will begin to act differently, make better choices, and ultimately

38

create new habits for yourself, because its habits that conserve your energy.

In order that you don't get too overwhelmed with trying to change too much too soon, go easy on yourself, sneak up on your body and mind slowly by taking small steps. On my own journey I began by using self –hypnosis.

Self –Hypnosis

I feel I need to share with you a bit about how powerful you really are. When you just awaken and when you are about to fall asleep, your brain waves are in alpha –theta mode, which is a highly suggestable state of being. A state we work with when doing Hypnotherapy. It is also a similar state that we are in when we are children under the age of six. Our minds are like sponges, easily absorbing everything we're told, without too much resistance or critical evaluation from our conscious minds.

You have a conscious mind and a subconscious mind which I explain about later on in more detail. But for now your conscious mind is the captain of your ship and your subconscious mind is the engine, directing you wherever you tell it go.

Whatever you say to yourself with feeling becomes your reality eventually. Even though you may be trying to say the right things, if things aren't t going the way you would like, it's because you haven't convinced your subconscious mind (the engine) that what you are saying is true.

The quickest way to make changes is by self -hypnosis, and by really feeling the feeling as if what you want to change, has already become a reality. So you concentrate on feeling relief, satisfaction, relaxed and so on.

How to do it

Find a comfortable place to relax where you won't be disturbed, close your eyes and breathe in and out slowly. I have a breathing technique which I repeatedly share throughout this book, you can practice that or make up your own variation of it.

Begin to think about how you would feel if what you wanted was already here in your reality, feels wonderful right?

Now repeat silently with feeling and satisfaction 'Success' 'It is done now, thanks,' 'I'm delighted.'

Imagine what way you would act from now on. If what you want is more money, then you must now begin to look at money different-ly. If you have a poverty consciousness, focusing on lack, then you need to change that to see all the abundance you already have and to practice gratitude.

I share various techniques like the Mind Movie throughout this book that will help you with this.

Only allow yourself to ponder on what you do want throughout the day, but most especially before you go to sleep and just as you awaken. It takes a bit of discipline and practice. You'll know you've managed to convince your subconscious mind, when you see things starting to change. As within in your mind, so without in your real-ity. It has to happen in your mind first.

Chapter 2

Thoughts

'Every thought is a battle, every breath is a war,
and I don't think I am winning anymore'

Unknown

Our thoughts create so many things, and most of us are just not aware of how powerful they can be.

I feel it is important to show you that your early chapters don't have to be the whole story. You don't have to continue to be the victim of your childhood or whatever experiences you've had. No matter what happened to you, it is possible to move on and create something better for yourself.

For most of my life, like most people I guess, I didn't know anything about thoughts, except that I had them. I didn't know that I wasn't my thoughts. I didn't know that I could change my thoughts. I didn't know that if I changed my thoughts that I could change how I felt, and could choose to feel good instead.

I didn't know that thoughts were energy, like radio waves. And I definitely didn't know that my thoughts could affect the world around me, and the thoughts of those people around me could affect me. Like a lot of people I was disempowered and running on autopilot trying my very best to cope and survive in the environment I found myself in.

Undesirable States of Mind

As I began working with my thoughts I realized that there were many kinds of thoughts. There were the limiting thoughts of I cant's, I'm not good enough, I'm not attractive enough or I'm too old. Then there were the rules in my head, the shoulds, the musts, the have to's. And then there were the thoughts of poverty consciousness, the fear of what others thought of me, depressing thoughts, anxiety building thoughts and so on, and on, oh my! Initially it was exhausting.

No wonder we are on autopilot, it uses less energy! But it's only because we have been programmed that way. It's kind of like, if you stitched a seam on a piece of fabric, and about a mile along, you realize that they are the wrong kind of stitches for what you wanted to create. So you begin to unpick them, and it's a bit of a pain in the ass to begin with, but soon you find it gets a little easier, and before you know it you're flying along. Well identifying and changing our thoughts are a bit like that.

Now it's not that when you're aware of your thoughts and you are choosing positive ones instead, that you won't get those other thoughts too. It's just that you'll see them as the Trekies would see Klingons on their starboard bough in Star Trek, and what would they do with them? Scrape them off Jim! That's it. I sometimes imagine a dumper truck on its way to the dump, and I send those unwanted thoughts there. You can use a bat and send them into a field, I got this idea from a book, Soul Psychology by Joshua Stone. I also say to the thoughts, 'thank you for the contribution, but I'll pass on that', or 'Not today thank you.'

From childhood you acquired a certain way of thinking that has affected you. Each thought, forms and strengthens a neural pathway and reinforces that way of thinking, which affects your behaviour, habits and beliefs. Some folk call them an ANT– Automatic Negative Thoughts. Well you can reverse that, it just takes some time. Aim to have a PET instead – Positive Encouraging Thoughts! How do you change them? One thought at a time darling, one thought at a time!

Thoughts Are Energy

Our world is made up of energy. We are made of energy and so are our thoughts. Energy cannot be destroyed it just changes form. Thoughts are like radio waves, we can't see them, but if we switch on a radio we can hear a voice. We are like radio receivers and radio transmitters.

The thoughts we have, affect our bodies, and affect our lives and relationships. They also have an effect on those we meet. And surprisingly those people around us can have an effect on us which can be positive or detrimental if we aren't aware.

I was having coffee with a friend a few years ago and we were discussing this. He didn't believe me, so I asked him to subtly give his attention to a man sitting with his back to us. I told him we would take turns, just looking at the persons back, just observing, but not allowing ourselves to be seen doing it, and not sending any positive or negative thoughts towards him.

The man we were watching began to get uncomfortable, he started looking behind him, eventually he made to get up and leave. I did feel bad about that by the way. My friend saw that we can have an effect on others by directing our thoughts or energy towards them. When you put your focus on something, you give it your energy. You don't want too many people like me around if you're running a coffee shop!

I read about another situation like this in the book, The Emotion Code by Dr Bradley Nelson. He demonstrates how a body can be affected by the thoughts that are directed at a person. He has a volunteer stand up with their back to a group. Behind their back he puts his thumb up for the group to direct a negative thought or a positive thought to the volunteer. By muscle testing he can then check if the person tests weak for the negative or strong for the positive, which they invariably do.

Why does that happen? Because from the Eastern spiritual perspective, we are all connected through Universal consciousness, energy, and what effects one, in some way affects all in varying degrees.

A word of warning, if you are directing negative thoughts towards anyone, including yourself, you are causing harm to yourself. Negative thoughts and emotions create acidity in the body. If the body becomes too acidic, the cells begin to react and think you are decomposing. Only dead things are acidic. Your immune system will begin to attack itself or you will become ill in some way. Positive thoughts and emotions create an alkaline environment in the body.

Interference, Thought Forms and Voices in Your Mind

Ok here comes some more 'woo, woo' stuff. Cue the music from The Twilight Zone!

If you view this with a sense of humour you'll get through it ok! Let's imagine for a moment that we have an angel on one shoulder offering us thought forms of who we want to be, or how we can be of service to others, how we can be kind and love unconditionally, how we can be empowered, or of how worthy we are, and a devil on the other, offering us thought forms of who we don't want to be, or how we can serve ourselves, how we can have power over and manipulate others, 24 /7, or how much doom and gloom there is and how we are just so unworthy.

Depending how we are orientated i.e. positive or negative, aware or unaware, one will be more appealing than the other, and if we are aware of this concept, then you need never be bothered by your thoughts ever again.

Now some of us are just too damned busy to be aware of our thoughts and some might be thinking that this is a load of bull, but stick with me for a few more sentences, or skip on further and at least try the breathing technique, and then you might understand what I'm saying. Of course you can still call this bull if you want, I don't mind really. A person convinced against their will, is of the same opinion still. I'm not trying to be right, I'm just sharing my truths. Your truth may be different. That's ok.

You have free will to choose your thoughts and your actions. Just because a thought form of a kind is offered to you, doesn't mean you have to entertain it or act on it. They have no power over you. No more than a radio channel has, if you don't like what you're hearing, change the channel. Just to note that while you have free will, you are not free of the consequences of harbouring thoughts or the actions you take. Your body is affected by everything, and also that's where Karma comes in.

I mentioned that we are like radio receivers and transmitters, and I mentioned Universal consciousness, and that thoughts are energy and that energy cannot be destroyed, it just changes form. So have you ever wondered where some of the thoughts or voices in your head come from? Yes some are self- talk, your own voice chattering away, observing, commenting, judging, arguing, criticizing etc. Some are replays of things your parents, teachers, or peers said, that have become your mantra.

But sometimes you might get to hear a little voice whispering a suggestion that you should say or do something. It might be an intuitive prompt, or maybe a negative prompt, and you may feel a bit disturbed that a thought like that could have arrived in your mind. Or you may find if you are in an argument, you may be prompted to say something that you know will emotionally wound the other person for example. Of course most people don't even notice this, they just act out without questioning. This is why it is extremely important that we become aware of our thoughts, so that we may become more aware.

I watched a video of Eleanor Longden: 'The voices in my head | TED Talk - TED.com,' about a woman who was diagnosed mentally ill. After hearing a voice in her mind that was initially a commentator on everything she did, other voices appeared which suggested tasks in exchange for help, or protection, which she acted on. That didn't work out too well for her. She believed later on when she was more balanced that the voices were a meaningful response to traumatic life events, particularly childhood events. She eventually qualified as a psychiatrist who is currently in a great position to help and support others. This is a concept which can help people. But what if all of those voices weren't just messages from her unhealed self or from her subconscious mind?

In the Western concept of mental health a person who admits to hearing voices in their minds and who sometimes feel compelled to act on those voices get diagnosed with schizophrenia and are either institutionalized, medicated, or and shock treated etc. Most people are never cured. Yet in some parts of the world this same person is considered a sensitive soul who has a gift of communication from other dimensions. They work with the individual throughout the craziness stage until they find the message that is trying to be communicated through them, often resulting in a cure. Check out this video on you tube called, 'What a Shaman sees in a mental hospital (https://www.youtube.com/watch?reload=9&v=1YTkeVXu3TM').

If your body is over producing dopamine in excess, you may even begin to hallucinate. There was research done on some schizophrenic patients back in the 1980's which after discovering the dopamine link, were given glycine supplements on a trial, a lot of them were cured. Certain foods trigger the chemical reaction of over producing dopamine, which can lead the person to suddenly start having a lot of negative voices in their heads. Diet is hugely important for all of us, as a proper diet which is mostly fresh or organic foods, will not produce the type of chemicals in our bodies that will leave us susceptible to experiencing this. Those foods also raise our vibration which I'll go into more detail about further on when I share about energy.

Psychics, mediums, shamans, channels and sensitive people can receive and communicate images and thought form messages from spirits of people who have passed over or can communicate higher wisdom from other dimensions, spirit guides, and ascended masters and so on. But I feel we all have the ability to receive and perceive things, and if we are aware or open to it, then it won't cause us problems. This knowledge is rarely shared openly and the secrecy surrounding this causes so much suffering for people.

I mentioned about us being like radios, transmitting and receiving. A lot of scientific studies have taken place which the general public is not aware of. A book of interest is 'Distant Mental Influencing' by

William Braud, Ph. D. They did a lot of research and testing to see if one person could affect another person mentally and physically from some remote distance, they also performed tests on remote viewing, to see if someone could mentally find a location and describe it by just giving coordinates. Someone even shook one person mentally and they actually felt it in another room! Another book about remote viewing and psychic abilities is 'Mind-Reach' by Russell Targ & Harold E. Putoff.

Ok so humans can possibly affect each other. Are some of the thoughts that arrive in our heads possibly coming from other people? Humour me. And what if other information in the shape of thought forms can reach us from other places? What if Angels, Spirit Guides, Dark Ones, Elementals, Thought Forms and other beings really exist in other dimensions? What if some are aware and unaware. Now I know this scares some people, because we have been brought up to believe that we are powerless mostly. But stick with me, I'll show you your power.

We see that there are things invisible to us which suddenly become visible under the correct microscope. These are the micro which can only be viewed through a microscope. All things have an opposite. The macro is? Could it be that there are dimensions and beings that we can't see? The macro scope to see them is a certain vibrational frequency that the more sensitive of those among us have. Scientists have proven that if something is moving at great speeds that it can become invisible to the naked eye. As something increases its frequency it can seem to not exist. Sound is another frequency, they have developed very high frequency sounds that are not audible with our basic hearing sense, but it can affect you.

In some places they banned the use of frequencies that would repel teenagers from hanging around outside of shops etc. No one, not even the teenagers could consciously hear the sounds, but it made them feel uncomfortable. There is currently the use of subliminal messaging in advertisements, children's films etc. Some have hidden messages in audio and picture forms. Do a Google search and you'll see what I'm talking about.

From a spiritual perspective which I'll share more about in another section, if you are of a low vibration and frequency, eating processed, sugary foods, harbouring negative thoughts and feelings like revenge, anger and resentment, being constantly stressed, using alcohol etc. you will attract more of the same frequencies. You will be more likely to attract negative thought forms, and be wide open to a form of psychic attack. I'll explain a bit more about this later on.

Your lower resonance will also attract people and situations to mirror your vibration. You may attract more drama and chaos. If your vibration and frequency is higher you will connect easier with higher wisdom and guidance, you'll begin to resonate with peace and harmony. If you don't know who you are spiritually, or if your mind is weak, and most of our minds are weak, because we have not been told who we are, then we can be interfered with. The media does it all the time.

As you raise your frequency and consciousness you're going to start affecting the world around you in a positive way. You'll be like a light, and unfortunately lights attract things like moths and insects and needy dependent people, and people and energies that want to dim your shine for various reasons, but you'll be better able to ward it all off with a state of love, not fear. It's better to know about this stuff, otherwise you might think you're going crazy. Now maybe you think I'm crazy, but I'll take that risk. This is a part of the Sacred Knowledge that has been hidden from most people over the centuries.

Most of us have an awareness of a conscience (the science of the heart) If we are tuned in, now and again we might hear a little voice saying oh don't do that, or perhaps suggesting something kind or nice, sometimes we listen sometimes we don't. But sometimes we can also hear a voice saying some not nice stuff, things like 'trip them up, slap them, I'll get them back' etc. Or a nasty comment about someone being fat or stupid.

There is a poem by Rumi that I'm reminded of so I'll share it.

The Guest House, by Rumi

This being human is a guest house.
Every morning a new arrival.
A joy, a depression, a meanness,
some momentary awareness comes
As an unexpected visitor.

Welcome and entertain them all!
Even if they're a crowd of sorrows,
who violently sweep your house
empty of its furniture,
still treat each guest honorably.
He may be clearing you out
for some new delight.

The dark thought, the shame, the malice,
meet them at the door laughing and invite them in.
Be grateful for whoever comes,
because each has been sent
as a guide from beyond.

Where does it all come from? I can't know for sure. A couple of people told me they kept hearing a voice saying to them when they were driving, 'go on drive into that other car and end it all'. And no they were perfectly normal with no mental health issues. They felt safe enough to share because of this information I'm sharing. They wouldn't normally talk about it. Nobody does.

From my knowledge of this, positive thought forms that may come from Angels, Guides, Wise Ones, Evolved souls etc. won't ever suggest that you do anything to harm yourself or others, they will never scold, berate or threaten you, they will never try to bargain with you, however the thought forms from the Dark Ones will, they offer you power, thoughts of doom and gloom, they'll persist in telling you that you're no good, they'll threaten the safety of your family if you don't do something etc. that's how you know the source.

This is the kind of thing the woman Eleanor mentioned experiencing. And yes this could also come from your lower self, your ego too.

I believe that we have a higher and a lower self (ego) the consciousness of the light and the dark is already within us. It's called duality. It's all a matter of which part you are going to tune into and entertain. Can I prove any of this, no, but there are a lot of people out there who have studied and written about aspects of this kind of thing. They can't be all wrong.

I knew a person who wasn't a racist. They found themselves in a shop queue behind another person of a different race. Their mind was suddenly bombarded with disturbing racist thoughts. When the person left, the thoughts went too. Were they picking up on that persons thoughts? Was there ancestral imprints in that person's energy field? Or was there a possibility that Dark Ones in the shape of thought forms, who never take a day off, were offering options?

Ok maybe you think this is all a bit whacky. But ask yourself will this information give you more freedom of choice. If you know that thought forms exist, no matter where they originate, and that some foods make it easier to experience bad thoughts, does this now give you more choices, more empowerment, than just asking a doctor for a pill to help stop all those disturbing thoughts and hoping it will all just magically go away? And a question for anyone on pills – did it work, or do the thoughts still come?

A person asked me once if it meant that they were a bad person if they kept receiving thoughts of a negative nature, worrying thoughts about the safety of their family, and all kinds of disturbing scenarios arriving in their mind. I said no, because they still listen to their conscience. If they were not heeding their conscience they wouldn't be upset with those thoughts and images, they wouldn't be feeling guilty about having them.

If fact they weren't that persons own thoughts, apparently they don't usually think thoughts like that, they didn't even invite those thoughts in, they arrived without an invitation. That person was the receiver of thought forms that came from who knows where. But this is the importance of knowing what is yours and what isn't. As you practice this you will become less disturbed by thoughts of this nature because you'll know the possible source of them and you can now accept or reject them.

If you read the poem by Rumi, regarding the thoughts, he suggests you welcome them all, by this I think he means to not allow them to disturb you. However my advice is to not ask the bad thoughts to sit down for a cup of tea with you. Don't entertain them. Let them come, you cannot stop them, let them in, then open a back door and show them the way back out!

Try this. If you focus on the centre of your chest (heart chakra) and gradually notice a feeling of warmth there, then imagine a feeling of love and light building up within you, encompassing you and then spreading out. Radiating all around you, filling the room, the neighbourhood, the country you live in, the world etc. You will raise your vibration to a different frequency, a different channel, so it will be more difficult for the negative news of doom and gloom and unworthiness of those thought forms to affect you.

You will notice them alright, but you can say 'pass on by' to them. Then you distract yourself by focusing on positive things. However if you identify with those negative thoughts, they will bring your vibration lower and lower to a place when you might seek solace in addictions or even decide to try to end it all. I made two feeble attempts to do myself in when I was in my early teens, and was strongly contemplating my options for a way out when I was at the end of my marriage, before I found all this information and started to practice it. It has made a huge difference. I don't entertain any negative thoughts now.

Some days I'm polite, I say feck off (in love and light of course!) to them. Other times I say return to sender and transmute to love, because some thoughts may originate in my subconscious, and I don't want to harm myself. I find I get less and less negative thoughts the more I do this. You can't stop thoughts from coming into your mind, you should know how important this is, a lot of people struggle trying to meditate looking to achieve a state of no mind. Maybe if you're a monk in the Himalayas surrounded by a lot of positive energy and high vibrational people you might be able to achieve this, but for most of us it won't be an easy reach in my opinion. If I get there though at any stage I'll let you know! I keep my sense of humour. I look at it like a menu of today's offerings, and I say 'I'm not having that today, or anytime soon either!'

Nothing or nobody has any power over you, except that you give your power away to them, whether in this reality or elsewhere. This is why it is so important to know who you really are and to be aware of your own thoughts. So that if somebody or something tries to interfere with you energetically on a mental level you will know what is yours and what is not.

We also live in a world of media manipulation that has us believing we are less than good enough, knowing who you are and what are your thoughts is your protection. I will also share about spiritual protection in another section. There is a very interesting series of books called The Law of One – The Ra Material, which mentions dimensional interference among many other things.

So whatever we believe to be true, we can't deny that we all have thoughts, some are good and some are not so good.

To change anything, first you've got to decide that you want to feel different, better and happier. You've got to want this more than the undesired state of mind, which is just a collection of thoughts. Second, you need to become aware of the types of thoughts you're having.

In order to become aware of your thoughts you need to be in a place of calm stillness and relaxation. You won't be able to focus amidst the chaos of everyday living. I'll just say briefly here that when we are stressed, hassled, upset, fearful, anxious etc. this triggers the reptilian part of our brain at the top of our spinal cord. It puts us into survival mode, or fight or flee. When this happens the oxygen that your brain needs in order to think clearly, travels out of your brain and down into your heart and lungs area. I'll explain more in the section about stress & anxiety, but for now here are some solutions.

PAULA O'SULLIVAN
Breathing Technique

Find a place where you won't be disturbed (ha, ha, ha, if you're lucky – lock yourself in the loo if necessary) Sit or lie down (not on the loo, I've never tried that but I don't think lying on the loo would work) A bed or a couch is best me thinks. Make sure you're warm and comfortable. Close your eyes, uncross arms and legs. Imagine that the breath is filling your chest and belly when you are inhaling. Your belly will rise. Placing your hands on your belly will let you know when you've managed this.

When you are exhaling, imagine that the breath is travelling out of your belly and down through your legs, feet and toes. Your belly will fall. Do it slowly and deeply, belly rise and fall. Do this five times or more. Breathing in calmness and relaxation, breathing out any worries or cares. Breathing in peace, breathing out love.

Or if you're not the love and light type of person, you can breathe in, thank God I got away from those feckers for a moment and breathe out, feck that shite anyway. Whatever works for you ha, ha!

Now that you're nice and calm. You are aren't you? Your brain has lots and lots of lovely oxygen and will allow the following information to be absorbed.

Did you know that there are two ways of thinking? These suggestions can be incorporated whether on medication or not.

The Two Ways of Thinking

The Worst Way: Most of us are stuck in this way of thinking by default. To remain in an undesirable state of mind we have to focus on all that is going wrong or has gone wrong, keep thinking negative thoughts, have thoughts of self- blame, perceived failures, have lack of faith in the future or have negative expectations.

We have to focus on the worst that could happen, to criticize ourselves and tell ourselves things like 'I can't', 'I won't cope' and 'I doubt it', which inevitably will lead to overwhelming feelings of despair, hopelessness, fear and lack of control. We have to not accept the reality of present, past or possible future situations. We play disaster movies in our minds and can't see ourselves coping. Seem familiar?

The Best Way: To escape the cycle of undesirable states of mind, we must begin to think in a better way. The best way focuses on accepting the reality of what has or is happening, even if you don't like it, and can provide you with some new questions to ask yourself. This way focuses on finding solutions.

Ok, so I don't like what happened or what is happening, or I don't know what will happen to me, but how best can I cope with that reality, right now, where I am, with what I have ?

What is the best thing I can do right now? And if there is no action I can take, how best can I survive right now?

Can I just accept what has happened without my needing to mentally control everything, can I just accept that some things can't be changed, validated or made better?

What is going right? What do I actually have right now?

When we ask our minds the right questions, it opens the door to our subconscious mind, which has all the answers. You will find yourself picturing yourself coping in the best possible way. You will ask yourself:

'How do I want to be feeling, coping, living?'

What would that feel like?

Is there anything I can do, no matter how small, to help me feel like that now?

How can things get better than this?

How would my life be different if I wasn't depressed or having these thoughts? And could I handle that?' This can provide surprising answers. If there is something you can't deal with in your life, the body will perceive that as a threat to the balance of health.

It will express that threat in some way, ie depression, illness, anxiety, pain etc. It's like the dashboard warning light in a car. It's drawing your attention to something in your life that needs to be dealt with.

Change the way you think about the situation, and you can maybe reverse the symptom. Sometimes we do too much damage and may not be able to repair it, but we can certainly still make conditions better than they were. Eckhart Tolle says in his book, The Power of Now, 'Change the situation by taking action or by speaking out if necessary or possible; leave the situation or accept it. All else is madness.'

Thoughts Create Your Reality

I think it was after reading the books 'The Secret' by Rhonda Byrne and Louise Hay's book 'You Can Heal Your Life' that I began to understand that our thoughts create our reality. Up until that point I was an unhappy victim, blaming my parents, my husband and everyone else for the way my life had turned out. When you blame, you don't accept responsibility for the part you've played. We are all responsible in some way. Don't scream at me just yet, hear me out!

Most of us don't realize how powerful we are. Look around you. This book was created first in my mind, with my thoughts before it became a reality. Cars, computers, clothes, your phone, the chair you sit on, the room, the building, the roads, pathways and so on, all were created in someone's mind with their thoughts first. Everything gets created twice. First in the mind and then a person takes action and the idea is created in reality. That's easy enough to understand. But what about where you are in life right now, in your study, career, or relationships?

Each thought we have, leads us to make a choice, which either leads us nearer or further away from what we really want to experience. You are now in this moment exactly where your past thoughts have led you. For some people this can be a scary realization.

A lot of us are not aware of our thoughts, or the underlying needs we have that direct us unconsciously to make the choices that we do. Most of the early thoughts I had were all based on fear. Up until the time I was ill in 2009 when I was 44, the choices I'd made unconsciously were to stay in emotionally abusive relationships again and again. I was afraid of being alone, I was afraid no one else would have me.

I married out of fear that I was getting too old (I was only 32!) I stayed in jobs I didn't like just because I had a mortgage to pay. I didn't try to achieve anything more because I was afraid of the responsibility if I was successful. I couldn't see past the next moment. I couldn't see myself doing it. It was all only fear, which is False Evidence Appearing Real, but that's the power of your thoughts for ya!

There is great freedom to be found when you become aware of your thoughts, and free yourself of fear based needs that colour your choices. After I learned that, I made better choices. I'm a work in progress though, always will be.

I don't think there's a point where you really 'get there' well not for long anyway. The point of humans and all nature is to evolve or die (mentally, physically, emotionally and spiritually) If you're not growing, then you must be dying. I was dying inside until I changed my thoughts.

Mind Movies

Most of our misery is linked with our thoughts and feelings. I mentioned how if we change our thoughts, we can change how we feel. Most people think it works the other way around. They feel unhappy, dissatisfied, angry, sad, depressed etc. and they wait for the feeling to pass, and it may or may not. Being aware of the types of thoughts though, at least offers you a choice in the matter. Oh I'm not saying this is going be a fast and easy thing for you. We all have good and bad days where we're more or less able to deal with stuff. Checking our thoughts can be tiring. But choose a day when you feel up to it, and then begin.

So when you become aware of your thoughts and how they may be affecting you, the next thing to become aware of is the images in our minds. Most of us have been conditioned to play disaster movies. We can't picture ourselves coping, or of things working out for us.

It is important to know that we can only really control the actions, behaviours and thoughts of ourselves. We all have free will. We live in a society that encourages the concept of external psychology. If someone isn't doing what we think is the best for them, then we go about finding various ways to supposedly encourage, bribe, punish, reward or manipulate them into doing what we want them to do. This isn't about that. However later on I will share with you how to raise your energetic vibration, so that you will start attracting different experiences. But it must begin within yourself first. As within, so without.

This is about becoming the actor in your own play. Only consciously. You're already acting, we all are. The problem is the script we're reading from was given to us before we were six years old. And some of that script is causing us pain and dysfunction. So we need a new script. Most of us are not aware of any of this. Think about it. Everything appears in your mind first before it becomes a reality. Before you go to the shops, work, and interview etc. Your mind plays out scenarios for you. Sometimes it can be torturing if you have anxiety or depression as you try to put all the pieces together before you step outside the door.

You try to see yourself meeting or interacting with people or situations. 'If I see her, I'll say this', if this happens I don't know how I will cope', then an imaginary conversation begins in your head. Some days you'll even talk yourself out of the experiences, because you couldn't see yourself doing it. A lot of it is to do with feeling fearful, but it doesn't have to be that way. You will only be able to do what you can see yourself doing.

Like a lot of people with anxiety and depression, I really suffered from overthinking everything out in the minutest of details. I had to have a clear picture of everything that would happen or how I would deal with it, before I could go out. Some days I even changed my clothes several times before I went out, I just couldn't accept the way I looked or felt. It was impossible! It was exhausting!

I'll share a little exercise for you to create positive mind movies instead of the disaster movies. Write down how you do want to feel. Do you want to feel calm, relaxed, and confident? What do you want your life to look like and how do you want to see yourself coping with whatever happens in your life?

Be as precise as you can. But make sure you write down something like 'I am calm, relaxed and confident in all situations', ' I can see myself coping in the best way I can' for example. Instead of writing I don't want to be like this or that. Words are very powerful, its better practice to focus on what you do want, not what you don't want.

In the early days of practicing this, I would often call up an image of myself as a strong survivor, admittedly sometimes it was of me standing on one plank, barely afloat, with one arm waving a flag, but hey I was still standing, I was still here! We need to keep our sense of humour!

I then moved on to create a very different life for myself. A life in which I became confident, became free of depression, and anxiety. Regained good health. Was happy in my own skin. A life where I could think for myself, be free of fear and worries, be able to be free of the limiting opinions of others. A life where anything was possible if I put the work in. A life where if I wanted to do or try something new, that I could easily train my mind to help me to see myself doing it. Which then made it less scary to actually take some action in the direction of where I wanted to go.

Now at this stage the little niggling nanny or granddad that is inside us all and who loves to doubt, will come out for a chat. It will tell you that this is a load of crap, and that you have better things to be doing and so on. This is a good moment to thank them for their contribution, to acknowledge their positive intention of protecting you from being fooled.

Just ask them to step aside for a few moments and to just observe. In order to get a different result you know you'll have to try something different, and this is the something different. They can give you their opinions after you've tried this out for yourself. I'll explain more about this in the section called Parts Therapy.

As adults we've been programmed to dismiss the power of our imaginations. We think it's a waste of time. Yet it has been proven scientifically that our bodies and subconscious minds don't actually know the difference between reality and imagination. Also in the battle between reality and imagination with regards your subconscious mind, your imagination always wins! Anything that affects you deeply becomes the hidden programme in your mind.

In an experiment, they tested athletes in different groups. Some sat around with eyes closed and imagined they were performing. Others performed, and the third group performed half of the time and imagined they were performing the other half of the time. The results showed that physiologically the same muscles reacted in all groups whether the person was sitting on a chair imagining, or actually out there doing it! Their performance results showed that those groups that trained and imagined perfect performances had the greater success. Your imagination is powerful, now let's start using it for your benefit!

Creating Your Mind Movie

Close your eyes, imagine that you are going into your own private movie theatre, you are alone and you are perfectly safe. Find a seat. Choose a scenario that you want to be or feel better in. How do you want to see yourself acting? How do you want to feel? What do you want to look and sound like? Now look up at the screen. You notice a freeze frame of a scene with you on the screen. Now press play and practice seeing, feeling and hearing the new you. Press pause, think of anything you want to change or improve. Then rewind the movie fast, pause and play the new scene. Repeat this at least three times and then press save.

This will take some time to get used to. Just keep practicing. Anytime the disaster movie or an image of what you don't want comes on in your mind, eject and play the new movie instead. Keep improving on what you want. If you can see it in your mind then you're already halfway there. When you are comfortable with what's in your mind, you can then start to practice it in your life.

Affirmations

Another thing I found useful were affirmations, short positive sentences, like 'Each and every day, I get better, and better in every way', 'I am whole, perfect and healed,' I am doing the best I can with what I know now, and when I know better I'll do better,' 'I'm in the process of becoming whole, perfect and strong, harmonious, healthy, wealthy and happy.' I wrote them out on post it notes and stuck them everywhere. Every time I started to feel a bit low, one of them would catch my eye, and remind me that I wanted to feel better, and I would imagine feeling what I wanted to feel.

It's really important that you conjure up the feeling. What feeling will you feel if what you are affirming is true? Will you feel relieved? Will you feel relaxed? Will you feel satisfied? Then feel that. I repeated them a few times when I awoke, during the day and again when I was drifting off to sleep. This is your body's natural hypnotic state, your mind is in alpha theta brainwave, and is very susceptible to suggestion, so be kind to your mind at these times!

I still use affirmations, they are great especially if you become aware of persistent thoughts arriving that don't make you feel good, say 'thanks for the contribution, but I'm choosing to feel worthy, happy, brave' or whatever. Choose a favourite sentence to have at the ready to counter any negative or self -defeating thought that arrives.

I've also found that just repeating one word with feeling, over and over prior to sleep, when I awaken and during the day can bring about some amazing results. Try just saying 'Health', 'Wealth', 'Success', for example.

I mentioned resistance earlier, it's when your conscious mind states something, but your subconscious mind doesn't accept it as true, because they are vain repetitions, without the feeling. So you find that what you are affirming doesn't work, and sometimes you seem to be worse off than before. If this happens just use those singular words and feel the feeling, this will not cause any resistance.

So choose your thoughts wisely. I read somewhere that you don't have to invite every negative thought form to come in and live rent free in your head!

Chapter 3

Two Minds

I guess now would be a good time to tell you about your two minds! We have a conscious mind and a subconscious mind. As mentioned earlier the conscious mind is like the captain of a ship and the subconscious mind is like the engine. It's not actually two minds but different levels of the same mind.

The conscious mind is what you use to filter information. It's the part of your mind that uses logic and reasoning. It can focus on approximately five to nine things at the same time. Think about the tip of an iceberg. The conscious mind holds some memories. It helps us live day to day and make plans. You cannot change things with logic. If you have deep patterns of undesirable habits and behaviours you need to reach your subconscious mind. That's were all the programmes are stored.

The subconscious mind can tackle approximately 30,000 things at the same time. It automatically controls your breathing, heart rate, digestion, blood flow and cell repair etc. Think about the part of an iceberg that is under water. The subconscious minds holds all memories and beliefs including those from any past lives or any imprinting between lives. It will block out anything that would be too much for you to handle. It is the genie in the bottle, your wish is my command. It doesn't know the difference between real or imagined. It just takes orders.

If you believe something very deeply and actually feel the feelings as if it were real, this is the part of your mind that can create that for you. Have you ever driven down a road with your mind full of thoughts of something and suddenly found that you had arrived home? Well the subconscious mind was able to get you home without you being very conscious about it.

When you're on auto pilot doing things that you repetitively do, then that's your subconscious mind helping you.

Imagine how tiring it would be for you if you had to be very conscious with everything you do all the time.

Emotions are held in the subconscious mind and can suddenly flare up out of nowhere if you are not conscious about it. I will mention about the emotional pain body, and also about releasing trapped emotions a bit later. Have you ever just reacted and wondered where on earth did that come from? Well it was hidden in your subconscious, unhealed and waiting to be triggered. It was a message.

Because everything is made of energy, vibration, frequency and resonance. If you perceive your life experiences as reflecting back to you that you are not good enough for example, then over time that will seep down deeply into your subconscious mind. This then creates a programme and an energy resonance which will begin to attract people and situations that are on the same energetic level.

I mentioned this briefly at the start. Have you ever noticed any patterns in your relationships? Have you ever looked back and noticed that it's been the same old story repeating over and over? For me it was always the same, I kept getting involved with people who abandoned me, they were all emotionally unavailable. Same kind of situations, just different players in the game of life.

66

It took me a long time to realize that I was abandoning myself first, I wasn't there for me. Later on I realized I had lots of layers of trapped emotions which had a resonance of abandonment and betrayal. Since I've done work on myself, I've become much more aware and able to discern the types of people who are also not there for themselves. To get into a relationship with them would mean that the pattern continues, so I am now able to avoid them. But this wouldn't work if I hadn't stopped abandoning myself, I would continue to be attracted to them.

There's a story about a snake in a desert. He's slowly drying out in the sun and needs to get to an oasis soon. A man passes by and the snake asks him in a shaky voice, 'Please sir can you carry me across the desert.' 'Ha, ha' says the man, 'you don't fool me, I know that if I pick you up, you will bite me.' The snake replies, 'on my honour sir, I won't bite you, please bring me across before I die in this heat.' He continues to plead and the man eventually feels sorry for him, and carries him across. As they reach the oasis and the man is putting the snake down, it bites the man. 'What did you do that for, you gave me your word of honour?' says the man, outraged. The snake looks at him pityingly and says, 'I'm sorry sir, but you knew what I was when you picked me up!'

Yes we can be fooled. The last few snakes didn't get to stay very long in my life, that's all I'll say.

In order to change anything you need to use repetition. Do you remember being in school and learning things over and over? Did your parents or guardians keep telling you things over and over? With hypnosis you can reach this part of your mind and re-programme using repetition and emotion. You can also use self-hypnosis, as mentioned earlier, but I'll say it again.

When you are drifting off to sleep or just about to awaken, you are in a naturally hypnotic state of awareness. Your brain is in alpha - theta mode. A highly suggestable state.

Focus only on those things that you would like to show up in your life at those times. In the past when I was ill, I focused only on health, seeing myself radiant and glowing, I affirmed that I was 'whole, perfect and healed, thank you.' I felt what it would feel like to have health.

I had an experience a few years ago when I was out walking, when a woman I passed had commented on how fit and healthy I looked, so I kept repeating this image and hearing her voice telling me this, over and over. Then during the day I reinforced all this. I listened to hypnosis on cd to help me to relax, and I paid attention to my diet and exercise, and I recovered very quickly, every time. I've done this for a lot of things.

Reconciling Conflicting Parts (Parts Therapy)

Have you ever been in two minds about something? Besides from your conscious mind and your subconscious mind not being in harmony with each other we also have within us aspects that are like parts or sub personalities that help us to organize our internal experiences. They all have a positive intention but sometimes they conflict. Have you ever been torn between the need to work and the strong desire to play? Or perhaps you had or have a habit like smoking which you really want to quit, but a part of you won't allow it?

We are primarily motivated by a promise of pleasure or a fear of pain. Every behaviour or habit that we've created has a payback. We wouldn't do anything unless it is serving us in some way. In simple terms we're getting something from it that we think we need. Sometimes though this can cause us problems in our health, or in our work life or relationships as we procrastinate and leave things to the last minute to deal with.

In NLP there is a term called 'reframing' that I've used on myself successfully over the past few years. I also learned about this when I was training as a Hypnotherapist, we called it Parts Therapy.

Basically you separate the problematic behaviour from its positive intention.

• Find a quiet space for yourself, you close your eyes and breathe slowly, and then you ask for the part of you that is keeping you stuck to communicate with you. You ask it what is it trying to communicate with you or what is it trying to do for you in a positive way? What is its positive purpose? It's handy to write these things down so that you can contemplate them after.

For example you want to quit smoking but can't seem to. The positive intention of smoking may be to help you to relax, to help you to think clearly, to reward you, to give you an escape clause when things are getting too much.

• Now ask to communicate with the 'creative' part to come up with three new ways to meet the needs of the positive intention. For example is there any other way you can relax without having a cigarette? Perhaps you could use the breathing technique I mentioned earlier instead. I'll explain more in the section about quitting smoking how this helps. Some people are now using vape pens, which in my opinion are much worse than cigarettes, you're only swapping your poisons.

Is there any way you can do something else that helps you to think clearly, yes the breathing technique will do that for you also. As for finding an escape clause when things get too much, is it really so difficult for us all to just say to someone, 'I just need some space, some time out to think and get some fresh air, I'll be back in a moment?'

If the creative part hasn't come up with suitable suggestions, go back and ask if it can come up with another three.

• After you've done this ask to communicate with the 'responsible' part for the problematic behaviour, ask if it accepts the other possibilities. If it doesn't then go back and find more options.

• Finally you ask yourself if there are any other parts that don't agree with this plan of action. If there are any objections, go back and find the part involved and find its positive intentions, and then seek other possible choices to meet those intentions.

Sometimes there are more than one part in conflict with each other, so you may have to try to negotiate between them.

• Ask to communicate with the two parts that are not in agreement with each other. Perhaps get a piece of paper and draw a line down the middle. Give each part a name and write them down on each side of the page.

• Find out what each parts positive intention is and what their overall intention is.

• Try to get the parts to converse with each other in order to understand the viewpoint of the other, and to appreciate the contribution and value that the other is offering. This is not a debate but a discussion. It's to find agreement between the two.

• For example if one part wants to work and the other to play, then a compromise can be reached if some work gets prioritized for a certain amount of time then some time can be planned for play. Or the opposite way around. I sometimes do it that way.

• Make sure that both parts are happy with the new choices and then check if there are any other parts that don't agree, then find their positive intentions and repeat the process.

* * *

There's a part of me that craves sugary foods when life gets stressful. This part of me just wants to reward me when things are tough. I was ok with this as I was keeping a balance between healthy foods and a treat. After a while though I started to get inflammation and pain in my hand.

Some foods produce histamine, and stress can cause a chemical reaction and produce more histamine in the bloodstream. This causes pain and inflammation. So I had to have a talk with myself! To just give it up would cause inner conflict, which might create some other health issue. I was aware that I was doing everything I could do to manage my response to the stressors in my life, but like most people I like a reward when life is being challenging. It helps me cope. We can't give everything up, then there's no joy!

I agreed with the part that wanted me to be rewarded, that yes I do like a treat but that I don't like inflammation and pain very much. So we looked for a positive solution. We decided to just have a treat a little less often than I was having them, and that I would choose to use my will, to decide when the urge came whether to have the treat that day, to delay it until later or to wait until another day. This way it wouldn't be compulsive, I would be aware each time that there is a choice in all of this.

I know this can sound ridiculous, but have any of you tried to seriously give up something and found it hard to do it? I was honest with myself, I didn't want to give it up completely.

If I told the part of me that wanted a reward, that I was going cold turkey and giving up forever on sweet stuff, there would be resistance, what you resist, persists. Oh I have stopped many things immediately, but I was in the right emotional space to do that at the time. The stress I was dealing with was ongoing. So this was a bit trickier for me.

In this way I acknowledged the positive intention of that part of me that was trying to look after me, and I didn't disrespect it. I said earlier that you have to sneak up on yourself. This is what I did. I didn't commit fully to giving up the sugar, but I also didn't agree that I would take it every time I felt a bit stressed either, which is what was happening. So the part of me that wants to be pain free now has a greater sense of awareness and choice and there is no conflict within me about it, and no guilt trips either.

Self – Talk

'You have been criticizing yourself for years,
and it hasn't worked. Try approving of yourself
and see what happens'

Louise L. Hay

I thought I'd share a bit more about self-talk as I mentioned it briefly earlier on and I feel it's really important to know about this. What is

Self-talk? It is the inner voice in our minds which provides us with a running commentary on everything in our lives. It is your own voice, or can be a parents, teachers, friends etc. It can be either positive or negative.

A lot of our self- talk developed in early childhood based on the things we heard others say to us and about us, or the things we observed others saying in general. We were young and impressionable and we believed what we heard. We formed unconscious agreements in our beliefs about ourselves (a belief is just a thought we keep thinking over and over) we become who we repeatedly tell ourselves that we are.

When I was feeling depressed I told myself many things that kept me down, unhappy and sometimes even suicidal in my earlier years. I constantly criticized myself and told myself over and over that I would fail, that I was no good, not worthy, stupid, ugly and fat. My mantra was 'I can't'.

As I've mentioned already, to change anything we must first become aware of where we are. We have to catch ourselves thinking, we have to listen to the inner dialogue. We have to talk back and say 'No, I don't agree with that anymore, that's my old conditioning, that's something my parents/ friends/ partner/ teacher etc. used to say, and that might have felt true for them, but it doesn't feel true for me, I want something better for me now!'

I discovered a RUT, was only a Record of Unhelpful Thoughts! I learned to not believe everything that I thought, and that by thinking different thoughts, that we can create different beliefs. In creating different beliefs we can change our habits and behaviour, and hey, there is one big exciting world out there waiting for us when we do this.

Want to feel better in yourself?

• Listen to your self-talk.

• Is it supportive of the person you want to be, or the life you want to have? If not, challenge it and change it, one thought at a time.

• If you're calling yourself 'stupid' for example, say instead 'No, I'm not stupid, I'm just doing the best I can with what I know now, and when I know better, I'll do better and I won't do it that way again after this for sure!.'

• Balance the talk, if you hear yourself saying 'There are no jobs out there' say instead, 'There are plenty of people working in the type of jobs they like, I'm just finding it a little bit difficult to find one that suits me, is there anything I can do, training etc. that would give me a better chance? If not what else can I do with the free time I have?'

• When you say something to yourself, ask if there is any evidence to support that thought, are you just assuming, is there another perspective to view this from? Would you speak to a friend the way you are speaking to yourself?

• Ask, 'Is this thought serving me, will it bring me to where I want to go in life, will it make me feel better or worse?'

Beliefs

You'll keep hearing about beliefs in this book, and that is because they are so powerful and they will attract into your reality their likeness. I'll be repeating this a lot, a belief is just a thought you keep thinking over and over, that's all it is.

74

Thoughts seep into the subconscious and create the right energetic frequency and then you will experience that as your reality. Grand so if your life is as you want it to be, but you're reading this book, so maybe all is not as you would wish it to be?

I've read so many stories about beliefs and it's scary. I read once about a man who worked on the railroad carriages in America, I think this was included in one of Jack Canfield's books. It was a Friday evening and all his buddies were heading off to a party, he was the last to leave and was just checking one of the refrigeration carriages when the door swung shut and locked him inside.

He knew all about what could happen, he knew he would freeze to death, alone, and wouldn't be found until the Monday morning. No one heard him call out. He was found dead on the Monday, frozen. He had managed to scrape a goodbye note to his family. The only thing that baffled everyone, was that the refrigeration carriage hadn't been connected to any power, so there was no explainable reason as to why he froze to death. Except that he had a belief that he would.

I read another about a man who was weary walking in the country-side and found an abandoned locked cottage to stay in overnight. During the night he got up in the darkness to open a window, which he couldn't so he broke the window and got lovely fresh air in the room. When he got up the next day though, in the daylight he could see that he had merely broken a glass door on a bookcase. Where did the air come from?

I've read stories of people who were told they only had a certain time to live, and who died promptly, only for it to be found out later that they had been misdiagnosed.

When I had a car accident in 2016, a paramedic put a line in my arm and told me I would get a pain killer soon. My pain was at an eight on the pain scale, when asked about 20 minutes later where my pain was at I said a four, as if the pain killer had worked. I was told I hadn't been given one. I was in shock and I had been trying to reduce my own pain levels mentally as best I could, but I think it was the suggestion that I would get a pain killer, that acted as a placebo, my belief that the pain would reduce worked. Being in shock is similar to the trance state of hypnosis. I laughed so much at having experienced that. Powerful!

This is the power of belief. Of course a lot of us wouldn't have experienced anything so dramatic in our lives. But our beliefs are shaping our experiences none the less.

Core Beliefs

I tried so hard in my early life to get somewhere, to be a 'somebody', but I always found that I could only get so far and then I would grind to a stop. It just all reinforced my beliefs that I wasn't ever going to be good enough. I had 'failure' tattooed invisibly to my forehead, which I could see every time I looked at myself. It wasn't until I discovered about core beliefs that I began to change this dismal view of myself.

So how is your life? Do you find that you begin with the best of intentions to change something, but find yourself at the last minute giving up or sabotaging it? Do you often tell yourself things like 'I'm worthless' 'I'm unlovable', 'I'm not good enough', 'I'm boring', 'I'm abnormal', 'I'm ugly', 'I'm stupid', 'I'm undeserving', 'I'm a bad person' or stuff like that ?

If you're not experiencing life as you'd really like to experience it, you may have acquired some unhelpful core beliefs. In fact to be perfectly honest, most of our misery is linked with our thoughts about things. 'Change the way you look at things and the things you look at change' – Wayne Dyer quote.

Core beliefs are the deeply held thoughts that influence how we interpret our experiences. They are the lens through which we view life. They will also determine how we behave. An example: A person with a core belief of 'I'm not good enough' versus a person with a belief of 'I am good enough'. You meet a new person and think of asking them to go out for a cuppa.

If you are viewing life through the 'I'm not good enough' lens, you will probably think 'Sure why would they even consider going out with someone like me, they'd probably prefer someone better looking, more educated etc….' the resulting behaviour is that you won't ask the person out, and you'll continue to feel not good enough.

A person looking through the lens of 'I am good enough' will have thoughts like 'Sure it might be fun, what have I got to lose, and if they say no that's ok, it's better to be in the company of people who really want to be with me anyway…' the resulting behaviour is that they will ask the person for a cuppa, and feel good regardless of the outcome.

Let's use another example, you want to apply for a job or a course. If you are looking through the not good enough lens, you will most probably talk yourself out of the whole idea before you even apply, most of my life was like that in the earlier years. You may say to yourself, ah sure 'I'm not young/ old enough, not educated enough, not intelligent enough' etc. If you do manage to apply and get it, you may talk yourself out of advancing. I did that too. I would scare myself, then leave a course or job and try again, and again, and again. I didn't get very far in those years.

I would apply eventually when pushed, mostly by my need to eat and keep a roof over my head. I would start the job, and my underlying core belief of I'm not good enough, would secretly announce itself to all around me. The people I worked with, subconsciously picked it up and worked overtime to mirror this back to me. I got bullied a lot in those days. I could never figure that out. I was a nice person, I was polite, I would do everything to help a customer, but the co - workers or sometimes the bosses seemed to want to bring me down to their level. Yet I never felt better than anyone.

I had low self-esteem, which makes you feel either inferior or superior. I definitely felt inferior. But they saw something in me that they wanted to crush. I left so many jobs in those days trying to escape this experience. It took me a long time to realize that change must happen on the inside first before it appears in our outside reality. We'll talk about that later on. If you are looking through the good enough lens, you will just apply for the job or course, if you don't get it and really want it, you might send an e mail requesting more information about what skills or experience you would need to be considered suitable and maybe apply again.

When we have a deep belief about ourselves we constantly try to prove we are right. We unconsciously make the people in our lives prove that we are good enough, that we are loveable etc. Of course they never will be able to, because we desperately need to be right, so it will all come around full circle, so that we can prove to ourselves that we are not good enough or lovable. I know, I know, it's a little fucked up, but that's us humans for you! The problem is the other person also has their own particular brand of shit going on too. Believe me when I say, if you can identify your core beliefs and change those that aren't working for you, your relationships will improve, with yourself and with others.

If you want to change some core beliefs here are a few suggestions:

• Keep a thought diary. Identify the things you say regularly to yourself.

• Remember that a belief is just a thought we keep thinking repeatedly. We form a subconscious agreement in our minds, and this in turn affects our thoughts, our behaviours, and in turn becomes a habit, which affects the decisions and actions we take or don't take.

• Look for the emotion involved, and look for the underlying fear beneath it.

• What are you afraid of? This can include the fear of been held accountable if you change, and the thought of being less accountable if you don't change.

• Notice and become aware of where you may be trying to control or influence another person's behaviour also, as we can only really have control and influence over ourselves.

Become aware of your thoughts that are upsetting you and choose the most dominant one.

On a piece of paper, ask yourself, 'If this thought were true, what would it mean?'

Ask 'Well what's so awful about that?'

With your answer now ask 'Well what does that say about me?'

Ask yourself 'Is this true all of the time?'

Now ask 'What experiences do I have that show that this belief is not completely true all the time?'

Ask 'What would be an appropriate, balanced and helpful core belief to have instead?'

Look for evidence that things may be different from your upsetting core belief.

If you practice challenging your thoughts regularly, you will change your beliefs.

Self-Esteem

'There is no magic cure, no making it all go away forever. There are only small steps upward; an easier day, an unexpected laugh, a mirror that doesn't matter anymore.'

Laurie Halse Anderson

I love that quote with the line 'A mirror that doesn't matter anymore'. It kind of sums up the result of building your self - esteem. I spent 44 years living with low self- esteem, where the mirror mattered and I really didn't like what I saw there.

The term 'Self-Esteem' refers to a person's general emotional evaluation of their own worth. It is an attitude and a judgment towards the self. It is all about the stories we create about ourselves.

We're not born with low self-esteem, but we enter this world very impressionable. Our minds are basically in theta brain wave mode for the first six years of childhood. This is a similar state we use in hypnosis for re programming (Alpha-Theta) in those early years, we easily absorb information from our environment.

Besides from the information you gather in those first six years, you may also have carried energy patterns from previous lifetimes that you are not aware of. But mostly it will be your experiences in this life time that will affect you. The love you did or didn't receive, will affect you. The way people treat you, the things they say, how you feel about it, will create your own personal script for life.

If you were not shown that you were loved in a way that was meaningful for you, you won't believe that you are lovable. If you weren't valued, you won't value yourself, if you weren't listened to, you'll believe that you have nothing worth saying, if you stick with the original script that is.

Now it is important to know, that those people in your early years also have scripts based on their early experiences. They were hypnotized and so were you. It goes back many generations. Most people are not fully aware of the hurts they cause to themselves and others, because they are trapped in the patterns of the way things were done back then and they have probably never questioned the programming. And I know I never questioned it until I arrived at the bottom of the abyss for the umpteenth time and realized that this wasn't a place I wanted to keep returning to. It was only then that the questioning began.

In Albert Villoldo's book 'The Four Insights' he mentions that as we grow up we soon become trapped in a triangle of disempowerment. We begin to identify with the roles of either Victim (powerless), Perpetrator (forcing issues) or Noble Rescuer (saving people) or else we're looking for someone to save or fix us. Have a look at your life right now, which role are you playing? I've played all these roles over the years, and the problem is, we begin to identify with them.

When I was a victim, life was unfair, it was out of my control, when I was a perpetrator I found I couldn't actually control everything, and when I was a noble rescuer, I found that if people really wanted to be saved or fixed they would do it themselves or would ask for assistance and actually take some action. I was also looking for a noble rescuer, to solve all my problems. I found this disempowering. The only person we can control is ourselves. The only person who can save us, heal us or fix us is ourselves, we are our own magic wand!

There is an underlying sense of insecurity in most of us that is never fully explained by psychology, and it has a lot to do with the concept of energy, which I'll elaborate on later. But basically we consciously or unconsciously play games to win energy which gives us a lift, in doing so we drain the other person. An example is when we are talking and the other person is listening. We have stolen their energy. If a person keeps interrupting, then they are trying to boost their energy levels by forcing you to listen to them. A child who repeatedly acts out is trying to get your attention and therefore an energy boost. There are many other ways we grab energy, but I'll include four that are mentioned in James Redfield's book The Celestine Prophecy.

When he talks about the control dramas, he mentions the 'Poor Me' – who takes energy by making others feel guilty and who complains about problems but isn't interested in solutions. This was my main one as I was growing up (victim) The 'Aloof' – Gets energy by being mysterious, vague and acts clueless, they keep retelling stories you've already heard. 'Intimidator' – Takes energy by threat, and forces your attention using fear. And the 'Interrogator' – Gets their energy by questioning and judging, in a fault finding way, and makes people feel inferior.

If you observe this closely you'll notice that if one way doesn't work, people will often snap into another drama or alternate between a few until they get the energy they need. It's very helpful to become aware of this. Later on I'll share how to build and maintain your energy without getting drained or having to play these games.

We also become identified with the roles of being a dependant, a parent, spouse, partner, sibling or with our job, our status, our possessions, our illness etc. etc. The problem is, what happens when your children grow up? Or you lose your job, a significant other, health or possessions? Does your sense of worth go too? Yes! Who are you without these things or people? Most of us tie up our self-worth in external things, and this affects our self-esteem, because nothing is permanent.

Everything is transient. The novelty of the new car, TV, partner, toys or clothes soon wears off and then we have to find something new to give us a new boost of worth. I'm reminded of the words of a song by The Smiths 'I was happy in the haze of a drunken hour, but heaven knows I'm miserable now, I was looking for a job, and then I found a job, and heaven knows I'm miserable now.'

To maintain low self-esteem, you will have to continue to identify your worth with these types of things, and you will have to constantly judge yourself on this. You will need to be critical of yourself and have negative self-talk. You will have to think that you are inferior or superior to others. You will constantly compare your performance, your possessions, and your abilities with others. Until the time that you become aware of everyone's uniqueness which is not comparable.

Also when you have low self-esteem, you will be broadcasting to the universe and all in it that you're not worthy. This is what happened to me. I had low self-esteem. I didn't feel worthy. I doubted my abilities, so everyone else did too. The people and situations I encountered mirrored back to me my doubts and fears, my own sense of inadequacy.

I didn't have the awareness that I do now, so I thought it was evidence, a reinforcement of my inner beliefs, of the 'waste of space' that I thought I was. But worse than the bullying, the belittlement, the emotional abuse I allowed myself to experience, was the situations I got myself into, due to manipulation by others, because of my unhealthy boundaries and my desperate need at those times to feel loved, accepted, approved of and my need to fit in.

Alongside my low self- esteem, I carried with me an 'emotional pain body'. I didn't know I had one until I read the books by Eckhart Tolle, 'The Power of Now' and 'A New Earth' a few years ago. Describing the pain body, Eckhart states, 'It is caused by the unconsciousness of the world into which you were born. This accumulated pain is a negative energy field that occupies your body and mind.' (*The Power of Now*, p 29)

In the past when I felt ignored or felt abandoned it would be a trigger for inner rage. The various situations or things people flippantly said to me that reminded me of my unworthiness, or my early childhood experiences of feeling unheard and emotionally abandoned would set me off. I would either withdraw quietly in pain and misery to the dark place within me that recognized my uselessness, or sometimes on rare unpredictable occasions I would shout and throw stuff around.

One time when I was in my early 20's, I broke something belonging to a partner I was living with, and he attacked me. It became a nasty physical battle as I awoke his 'emotional pain body'. I came out the worse of it. I had to wear long sleeves to cover the bruises. This attention although scary and painful somehow satiated my pain body as it just needed attention, even perversely negative attention. Anything was better than nothing. If neither person in a relationship knows about 'pain bodies', then it can get real dysfunctional.

Luckily it was a tipping point for me. I decided I never wanted to experience anything like that again, so I left the relationship as soon as I could. At that time in my life I didn't realize that it takes 'two to tangle', and that it is never just one person's fault when things go awry. In those days though I did a lot of blaming and fault finding of myself and others.

I learned from that experience and began to tame my responses, I choose to repress instead. I didn't know any other way to deal with these deep inner feelings and I certainly didn't want any more of my childish outbursts. This later accumulated unexpressed emotional energy within me and created an underactive thyroid and later on an MS / Lupus type illness, but more about that later.

Of course everyone is different, some express their emotional pain body, some repress, some become passive aggressive. 'Make them wait for me', 'make them pay', 'make them prove they love me', even though those unsuspecting people in your life will never convince you of a worth you don't believe you have, they will have to work hard constantly to try to prove it.

Yes I admit in the early years I was 'High Maintenance' until I realized consciously what I was doing and why. The problem with all of this is if you have an 'emotional pain body', you may not be aware of it, and it can and does trigger others, which can be damaging for all concerned. If someone triggers me now, and believe me this stuff is deep, it's not as bad now that I'm aware what's happening. I go home and work on myself, but it still surfaces now and again just to show me how far I've progressed, which is heaps compared to where I began.

But regarding the other person who keeps pressing my buttons, I detach myself from them in some way. An unconsciously unhealed 'pain body' in someone can be highly destructive. If that person has feelings of unworthiness for example, and you also have those same energetic resonances of unworthiness within you, whether you're aware or not, that person can trigger some sort of emotional pain in you, until one or both of you becomes aware of what is happening and take steps to heal it.

If you're taking steps to heal your wounds and they are not, the hurt will continue. To stay in their presence will only further damage you, no matter how much you love them. In the long term I found those kind of relationships are not worth it. They only drag you back into the abyss and stop your positive growth from occurring. I think that most people are mirrors reflecting back to us our unhealed selves, so that we can evolve and grow into a better version of ourselves. Unfortunately most of us aren't aware of this possibility, so we just keep hurting each other and ourselves.

Now if you do decide to take the route of building your self-esteem you are going to change your energy resonance, in short you're going to shine, you're going to switch on a light inside of you. The people around you who don't want to change themselves or their behaviours, who don't want to step up their game, so to speak, will be mightily pissed off with you. They will no longer share the same resonance of unworthy with you. You will seem different to them all of a sudden. They might try to bring you down to their level again.

I mentioned before about people trying to do this to me in work. I didn't know I had a light on already inside of me all that time, it was a something that shone, even though I felt unworthy, others recognized that I was different to them. Not better than, just different. Sometimes this light that you have too, even though you might be afraid of it, even though it may have been dimmed over the years, this light may ignite the demons in others. If you've had experiences like I did you'll know what I'm talking about.

I would only meet someone and I could see it in their eyes that I was in for it. I reminded them of something that they were not, or perhaps there was an essence of goodness that they didn't feel worthy enough to have achieved themselves, or perhaps I reminded them that they could be something better than they were, but they didn't feel able to get there. Though I didn't understand any of those possibilities at the time.

A few years ago, I was visiting my Dad in hospital. He had dementia. I was about a half hour late as I got delayed. I could only get down to see him once a week, due to responsibilities with my children, so I was really eager to greet him and spend as much time as I could before visiting hours ended. As I walked into the ward, there were some nurses dressing a bed beside the bed my father was in. Some of my family were already seated around his bed. The nurses had the bed pulled out slightly from the wall, and all I had to do was walk slightly around it to get to my father who was behind them from my view.

As I was about to do so, as I didn't want to get in the nurses way, or disturb them in their work, one nurse looked at me with that look in her eyes that I was oh too painfully familiar with. When I say a demon arouse in her, I'm not joking. I was quite shocked. She viciously swung the bed out in front of me and told me I couldn't pass. I didn't know whether to laugh or cry at the absurdness of it. I tried to reason with her, but she pulled the bed further out again, she was determined to stop me for some reason that I couldn't fathom.

It was really bizarre. After a few minutes of this craziness, in desperation, I raised my arms as if to touch her arms but didn't, and I raised my voice and said, 'Oh for God's sake let me pass, I have to see my father, and then I'll be right out of your way' and I just walked between her and the bed, and sat down on a chair behind her, while she muttered loudly in an angry voice about how these kind of people shouldn't be allowed in here! I was dazed and wondering like WTF was that all about.

Eckhart Tolle tells of a similar experience in his book The Power of

Now, where a man in a wheel chair went berserk and slammed into a waitress, because his pain body suddenly awakened not long after Eckhart had sat down to eat. Eckhart had previously been with a client who had a heavy energy around them and he hadn't cleared it from his energy field when he had finished consulting with them.

Now I don't know exactly why the nurse acted the way she did for sure, no more than I know about any of the others, maybe we had past lives together and I was mean to them, who knows, but whatever it was, after a long time I realized that it didn't mean that I was deserving of that treatment. I can't do anything about past lives unfortunately! I can only account for my behaviour in this one!

It was all back to them, the issue was their problem, not mine, and it was that they were just projecting the level of low self-worth or repressed anger that they had. Oh happy days when I realized that, for no one has been ever able to disrespect or bully me ever again. Oh some have tried, but they have been told that I don't accept that kind of thing anymore. I'm very direct nowadays and have much healthier boundaries.

Knowing all this, how do we turn it around and begin to build our self-esteem and tackle the enemy within?

• Become aware of your thoughts and choose alternative ones that make you feel good, that make you feel loved, valued etc. Low self-esteem needs to be fed with negative unsupportive thoughts. Stop feeding it.

• An emotional pain body needs to remain hidden to survive. Once you become aware of its existence, and catch it in the act, it will gradually lose its power over you. Just keep observing yourself without judgement. Just keep responding with a higher awareness.

• Develop positive self-talk if you catch yourself putting yourself down, focus on what you are good at. Do some core beliefs work to discover deeply hidden beliefs and emotions that might trigger a dormant emotional pain body.

• Write down the roles you've identified with, awareness is the first step towards changing something.

• Accept responsibility for the part you play, no more blaming, it gives our power away.

• Stop judging yourself, you're doing the best you can with what you know right now, and when you know better, you'll do better, and so will other people. You can of course tell them what you don't find acceptable, but you won't make them change. A person convinced against their will, is of the same opinion still, as they say.

• Don't tie up your worth in other people or external things. Find out who you really are without these things.

• Find things to like about yourself, and practice doing things that you enjoy.

• Stop comparing yourself to others. You haven't walked the same paths. You haven't had the same experiences. There is no such thing as inferior or superior. There is no such thing as an equal either! We are all unique beings with different strengths and weaknesses, that's all.

• Be patient with yourself, this takes time. Start creating a new you, decide who you want to be now and for the future, this will build your self-esteem. Remember it's all only a story we tell ourselves anyway.

• Keep a check on your boundaries from time to time. Disrespect starts in seemingly small insignificant ways. Texts or messages not replied to in a timely manner, promises not kept, keeping you waiting frequently, not paying back a loan, and so on. People will only treat you the way you allow them to treat you. If you don't speak up, they'll think its ok.

Mindfulness

I've incorporated this into my daily routine for the past ten years or so, at the time of writing this. The benefits of this are huge and life changing. Through practicing mindfulness 24/7, I've improved my health. I initially had a MS type illness back in 2009 which rapidly disappeared after practicing mindfulness, among other things like NLP, Hypnosis, Reiki etc. I'll share about this further on. I've prevented or in some cases shortened the life of colds which I rarely get anymore, and I've reduced pain and inflammation, I don't get as much as I used to. I don't tend to worry anymore, I'm not depressed and I overcame anxiety. I'm more present with everyone. My relationship with myself and others are closer and more authentic.

The word 'Mindful', means taking heed, or care, being conscious. And the word 'Conscious', means being aware and awake.

Most of us are not really aware or awake, we think we are, but we are really running on auto pilot, continuously being in a state of reaction or resistance. Mindfulness means paying attention on purpose. Being here and now with our present thoughts and experiences in a non-judgmental way.

Nothing is perceived to be either good or bad. It is what it is. Situations can be thought about in many ways.

We are like a boat without oars, being pushed this and that way, as life throws stuff at us. Our reactions are based on thoughts about past experiences, pre conditioned patterns from our early years or fearful thoughts of the future. Something happens that we don't like or want, and we set up resistance in our mind to it. When we resist something, our body and mind perceives this as a threat to the natural balance of things. We trigger the stress response which can impair our immune system, leaving us open to illness and disease and we also stop our minds from finding solutions.

When you become aware of your thoughts you will notice that we are either caught up in thoughts of the past or thoughts about the future. These are both areas where we have no control over, and this produces worries, fears, anxiety, depression and stress. We are rarely ever fully present, which can affect our relationships and health.

Our bodies give us clues that can help us have better health. With mindfulness, we can prevent some illnesses before they even begin. Pay attention to messages sent from your body, things like regular headaches, chest pains, stomach issues, frequent colds or illnesses. They are a communication from your body that things are out of balance. Your mind and body have amazing abilities to heal.

If you get cut, it will heal itself if you keep it clean, if you break a bone, it will heal itself if set correctly. Every illness has a cause, don't always ask 'what is the matter?' Consider 'who is the matter with you?' A lot of it is emotional based. 90 % of illness is psychosomatic, that means that your mind, body or spirit is out of balance somewhere. Illnesses are also caused by poor diet, lack of exercise, trapped emotions, toxins etc. It can be complex.

When we are stressed, anxious, angry, upset etc. the body perceives this as a threat, and the cells in the body shut off into a state of protection. They can no longer receive the stimuli they need. Your immune system gets compromised.

When you are balanced, the cells are in a state of growth and your immune system is working effectively. A good way to begin practicing mindfulness is through using a breathing technique which I mentioned in the section about thoughts. I'll include it here again.

Breathing Technique

Find a place where you won't be disturbed. Sit or lie down. Close your eyes, uncross arms and legs, imagine that the breath is filling your chest and belly when you are inhaling, your belly will rise. Placing your hands on your belly will let you know when you've managed this. When you are exhaling, imagine that the breath is travelling out of your belly and down through your legs, feet and toes. Your belly will fall. Do it slowly and deeply, belly rise and fall. Do this five times or more. Breathing in calmness and relaxation, breathing out any worries or cares. Breathing in peace, breathing out love.

* * *

My youngest son said to me a while back, that he noticed how different I was now compared to when he was younger. He said he couldn't explain what it was. He said I was nice back then, but he really liked it better how I was right now. The truth is I am present for him and my other son now. I was like a hologram back in their early years. I was listening to them without really listening. I gave the appropriate uh huh and hmmmms, the occasional nod, but I was only half with them. At that time my mind was tortured with thoughts of fear, depression and anxiety. My mind was full of lists of things to do next. And it wasn't just with my kids, I was like that with everyone. I tried my best but I didn't know any better.

Everyone has a basic need to be heard, and to be loved accepted, respected and valued, yet for many of us, we aren't really listening to each other, we are just waiting to reply. With mindfulness we pay attention to where we are interrupting or not listening, and we bring ourselves into the present moment and give the other person the sacred space to express themselves. Besides from being very annoying, when you interrupt, you're unconsciously telling the other person that what you have to say, is more important than what they are saying.

It is very powerful and healing when someone truly listens. Mindfulness teaches us to let the other person have their say first. When you speak first you are just repeating what you already know, by listening you will learn something new. Most of us are just seeking validation, we need to feel worthy. When we listen we honour that person in a sacred way. The amount of damage that happens when we are not truly listened to is monumental.

Very few people seemed interested in what I had to say from early childhood onwards. This helped me to feel unworthy, and so I stopped sharing my thoughts. I even stopped thinking for myself. Groups were the worst for me, I never got a word in edgeways. It was like I was invisible. I kind of got used to it, even though I didn't particularly like not being heard. In 2009 someone truly listening to me was a catalyst for my healing,

But before that I developed an underactive thyroid, which now that I am educated about the holistic side of illness, I see this as very relevant.

Our throats, throat chakra represent communication, speaking our truths and expressing ourselves creatively etc. Yes there are many more things that affect thyroid health which will be mentioned later on, but enough to say that after finding a way to express myself through my writing and speaking my truth, whether anyone reads it or not, and reducing toxins etc. I don't have any symptoms now, and I'm on a very small dose of Eltroxin and still have hopes of reducing it further and eventually hope to get off it if I can.

I highly recommend Eckhart Tolle's book The Power of Now, its well worth the read. Here's a little exercise for you inspired by his work.

Come into the 'Now' Visualization

Close your eyes and breathe in and out slowly five times. Notice any thoughts you have about the past. Place them in an index file for safety. Now notice any thoughts you have about the future or what comes next. Place them in an index file for safety. Now notice any thoughts that are not about the past or the future. If you have safely filed away the thoughts of the past or future, you will only have thoughts of the present. Most people though find a void of nothingness when they get to this point. That's your now.

* * *

Initially when I tried this and realized that there was nothing in my head when I was in the 'Now', I was a bit put out. All that nothingness was too much for me, or rather it was not enough. I could see why I was filling my head with thoughts of past and future, it passed the time. But then with practice I saw that what my head was actually filled with was causing me emotional pain, anxiety and depression, because past and future are things we have no control over.

However when we become mindful, then we can actually begin to create a bright new future for ourselves from the emptiness. Without past or future, by being in the present, we can decide how we would like to be from now on, and do the best we can with what we have right now. This is empowering.

I became aware that like most people I was filling up the nothingness with busyness. I was wasting a lot of time watching TV, soaps, crime investigations, the news, you name it. I was reading fiction that was also filled with violence and heartbreak. This added to my feelings of depression and anxiety.

So after practicing mindfulness for a while it sank in and I began a new way of being. I stopped watching TV altogether. I stopped listening to the radio. I stopped buying newspapers and reading stuff that frightened me. I started reading personal development, spiritual and metaphysical books. I listened to uplifting music. I watched uplifting movies and I've been doing that for 10 years now, with no regrets.

Tips for Being Mindful

• When you become aware that your thoughts are in the past or future, gently bring them into the present moment. Take a few slow deep breaths in and out. Notice your surroundings. Be kind and patient with yourself. Say 'I'm ok now in this moment'

• Develop a sense of gratitude. Say 'I have more than enough' Look for things to be grateful for. Roof over your head, food, clothes etc.

• If you're feeling angry, sad etc. do not judge the feeling, just observe it and say 'Oh here's comes anger, I wonder what brought that on?' In that mindful moment you have a chance to reflect or react in a different way than you did previously. Sometimes our reaction is based on some expectation of ours, or a need that hasn't been met, or it's an area where we have no control over. This can make us mad because it seems to make us feel like we are powerless, and our ego doesn't like that. Become aware of what is underneath your feeling and you will no longer be reacting on auto pilot. You will be free to choose your response.

• Do one thing at a time and be fully present with it. If you're drinking or eating, taste the food, smell it, notice the texture etc. When washing the dishes, feel the suds, see the rainbow colours. If you're out in the rain, look at the droplets on a branch, there's a tiny world reflected there. If walking, notice your feet connecting with the ground, feel the sun, or wind, warmth of your clothes, look at the sky. If with someone, listen carefully to what they say, really look at them, hear them. Be present.

• Listen to your body, what's it trying to tell you? If you've got a headache, ask yourself what was happening in your life prior to that? If you have pain, what is paining you in your life? What emotional conflicts have you not dealt with? What thoughts or emotions do you hold onto that might create pain for you. If you're depressed, feeling low or anxious, what are you resisting? What can you not accept? Who or what can you not forgive? Where is your life not meeting your expectations? Where do you feel you have no control? If you are getting frequent colds etc. your immune system has been weakened by stress, not nurturing yourself etc. Ignore it and other things may happen to draw your attention to where your body feels out of balance.

With mindfulness, we can become aware and rest before our body makes us. We can identify our emotional pain and reduce the chance that our body will have to give us a pain message. We can create new meaning in our lives and improve the relationship with ourselves and others.

Chapter 4

Overcoming Fear

We are born with only two fears, the fear of falling, and the fear of loud noises. These are there to protect our survival. If we have other fears, we have acquired them though our repeated dominant thoughts, the use of our imagination and through learned behaviour and response.

What is Fear?

Fear is a chain reaction in the brain that starts with a stressful stimulus which then produces the fight-or-flight response. The stimulus could be a spider, a memory, a thought, a feeling, or something else, which is a trigger for the brain to release chemicals, cortisol and adrenalin etc. which cause our bodies to prepare to fight or flee.

The oxygen in our brains travels very fast down to the heart and lungs area, and makes us breathe faster, blood and oxygen gets pumped into our muscles, arms and legs, giving us the strength to get away and survive.

When we think the same kind of thoughts, we engage our imagination, we produce the same kind of response in our bodies and minds, and we reinforce the fear. It's a cycle that can't be broken unless we change something first.

Learned Response

Observe any child under the age of six, if they hurt themselves, are faced with a situation, or see a spider for example, they will always look to the nearest adult to see how they respond first, before they respond. This is how we learn how to act, behave and survive in the big world we find ourselves in. Most of us want to fit in and belong, so we mirror the behaviours and reactions of those closest to us. In a way we form a subconscious agreement with these people, that this is the way to react and respond when this stimulus or situation happens.

Just to say if you don't react the same way there is usually huge peer pressure to conform to their way of being from those around you. This doesn't just apply to fears, it also applies to relationships, addictions, depression and so on. We can find ourselves as adults still playing the same old scripts that we agreed to when we were children, and it becomes our automatic response to things.

I grew up afraid to speak my truth, I was afraid of confrontation, because in my early childhood if I made noise I was punished. This kept me in some very abusive relationships for far longer than I cared to be in them.

I really struggled internally with interactions including making phone calls. Later on when I was married if I could avoid making a call and get my husband to do it instead, I would. I had fears about everything and I worried a lot.

In 2005 I became a sales manager with Avon Cosmetics and I got into the list of top 20 managers. I won a trip of a lifetime, a Caribbean cruise with spending money. But I still had fears and anxiety. I struggled and fretted and worried about going away from home for a whole week. I couldn't see myself going. I kept imagining every disaster. My husband didn't want me to leave him minding the kids. He knew of my fears. He finalized it by bringing home a film about a cruise ship that sank. Obviously I didn't go. I can see the funny side of this now, even though it's a sad story. It reminds me that if you are not in your own power then you can be easily manipulated. If you are fearful then people can and will use those fears against you if it suits their agenda.

So to change this we use a series of steps.

• Decide how you want to respond to future stimulus. How do you want to react and to feel?

• Use the Anxiety Breathing Technique on a daily basis to form a new habit in the body to prevent the stress response from triggering physiological changes. So that once your mind is calm the body becomes calm, and you can think more clearly.

• Then engage your thoughts and imagination, by acting out the responses that you do want, in your mind first. By thinking the kind of thoughts about what you want, you then get to feel the feelings that you want to experience. Practice playing positive mind movies (I'll include it again below) which will enable you to create the desired result. Switching over to this new mind movie, whenever your thoughts prompt you to play the fearful disaster movie instead. You have a choice which movie to play, you just need to become aware of it and choose wisely.

• The best time to do this, is last thing before you drift into sleep, and first thing when you awaken. Your mind is at a very high natural hypnotic state of awareness at these times. It will also work if you take naps during the day, do it before and after them. Don't wait until you are facing your fear again because you won't be able to tackle it in that moment. Start practicing now and you will be more able to cope with any future thoughts of fear.

• Remember danger is real, but fear is a possible response to perceived danger.

Creating Your Mind Movie

Close your eyes, imagine that you are going into your own private movie theatre, you are alone and you are perfectly safe. Find a seat. Choose a scenario that you want to be or feel better in. How do you want to see yourself acting? How do you want to feel? What do you want to look and sound like? Now look up at the screen. You notice a freeze frame of a scene with you on the screen. Now press play and practice seeing, feeling and hearing the new you. Press pause, think of anything you want to change or improve.

Then rewind the movie fast, pause and play the new scene. Repeat this at least three times and then press save. This will take some time to get used to. Just keep practicing. Anytime the disaster movie or an image of what you don't want comes on in your mind, eject and play the new movie instead. Keep improving on what you want. If you can see it in your mind then you're already halfway there. When you are comfortable with what's in your mind, you can then start to practice it in your life.

PAULA O'SULLIVAN
Disassociating Painful Memories

Most of us have experienced things that have upset us in our lives, whether in childhood, in relationships, or traumatic situations. First, try to accept what has happened. You don't have to like what happened in order to accept it. Your acceptance of the facts doesn't condone the actions of the people involved or the situation you found yourself in. This doesn't mean you're giving permission for this to happen to you again. Most of our pain and suffering, and in some cases depression, are caused by our lack of acceptance of what the reality is, and the thoughts and feelings we have about the situation. Your resistance if any will prevent you from healing, so these techniques help you to reduce the resistance.

If you accept that you can't change what has happened, but you'd like to change how you feel about it, then you can move on to disassociate effectively.

I like to remind myself that, 'That was then and this is now'. We only have a little time on this earth, and I'm not going to allow what happened to me, to suck all the joy out of me for the rest of my life anymore. I choose to move on.

What we're aiming to do here, is to emotionally detach, so that you're less identified or swamped, allowing you to be able to move on with a clearer perspective.

I found these techniques in various books about NLP, I used them at times when I had a lot of emotional healing to do, the first one I created myself to stop myself from developing post-traumatic stress disorder after a car accident, I've used them successfully on myself and clients.

After I was involved in a head on collision in my car in 2016. I noticed that my mind kept playing back the accident, but that it didn't stop with the facts, it decided to invite my imagination in for tea, and it brought every fecking scenario that could be imagined into the show. Before long there wasn't just scenes of the car that actually hit me, but there were buses and trucks, you name it.

Now those images if taken seriously will create a form of post-traumatic stress disorder, or other kinds of mental health issues. You receive an image in your mind, then your mind has to make some kind of sense of it, so it will assign a thought to make it meaningful, usually from your bank of collected usual thoughts that were imprinted from way back in your early conditioning and reinforced ever since. This thought will then assign a feeling, and off we go on a little merry go round trip.

Ok so it can go a little like this, I see in my mind a truck coming at me, my mind and body very painfully remember what it felt like when a real car crashed into me, the pain, the noise, the smoke, the shock, the confusion, the fear, the feeling I or my son might die, you name it. Obviously it was bad enough that I even had to experience that once, but here's my mind and it's just not content enough, it's stuck on rinse and repeat and I'm going to suffer worse each time it presents something like this, which it will keep doing, because it doesn't know how to shut it off until I consciously deal with it.

Each time my mind repeats this, it imprints everything that I don't want to think about and everything I don't want to feel, more and more intensely, it strengthens the neural pathways in the brain, so that if I allow this to continue, I will become like Pavlov's Dog in his experiments, who salivates every time it hears a bell when there isn't even a crumb of food in sight.

It creates an association. At this rate before long I would only have to go outside and see a car or a truck and it would bring back all the fear and even pain that I had originally experienced, only this would be far worse, there would be an extra layer of fear and terror that it might happen again. This could then create an anxiety so that I wouldn't drive again, or leave the house again, or could even begin an illness that would prevent me from having to face another possible situation ever again. The mind is incredible but potentially debilitating.

Thinking about this one day I began to laugh. I thought the only thing my mind had failed to create was dancing hippos on a circus scooter. Before long I was having a ball, the more ridiculous the better.

So I would wait until my talented imagination brought me another gift. Then I would change the image in my mind. I detached and became an observer. I mentally commented. 'Oh look here comes that ominous looking truck just about to hit my itzy bitzy car with little ole me in it. Oh no and there's a hippo in it, wearing a pink tutu, is that truck really pink and made of marshmallow? Maybe I was mistaken, perhaps it wasn't a truck that was coming at me, or maybe it was Ronald Mc Donald on a tricycle. Oh no it's a bus load of dancing hippos / monkeys/ flamingos.' Ok you get the idea.

I know this sounds too simple, and that you really want to be, oh so grown up like the world tells you should be, and that you really need to take your mind seriously, but I'm telling you, that you can be enslaved by your mind very easily. None of that stuff is real. The original memory might be real, but it doesn't take long for the mind to embellish. Listen to anyone telling a story about something, they'll nearly always end with something like, I could have been killed, or this or that could have happened. It's not bad enough what actually happens, our minds want to also focus on what could have happened too, which is almost always worse than what did happen.

This technique of swapping images if done consistently will break a pattern in the neural pathways, so that the automatic mental response to the images will weaken, as our thoughts create how we feel, you will then be able to change the feelings, and this will free you up to decide how you do want to be in future situations.

You can use this concept with a lot of situations. A young person told me of a recurring dream with a scary character that they remembered when they woke. I suggested they imagine the character in a bright red wig and an eye patch, then in a blonde wig with a daisy hairband, then instead of the scary black robe, how about a nice polka dot dress, blue or pink? Practicing this takes the intensity out of it and its fun.

Everything is just your thoughts and the thoughts create the feelings, and neither have any power over you, except that you give your power away. Your choice.

The following are just three suggestions, you can make up your own, use your imagination. Just don't imagine anyone getting hurt. You reap what you sow energetically. Everything returns to sender in some way, shape or form. It's not worth it.

Dancing Hippos

• Imagine a person or situation that is frightening or upsetting you.

• You notice that you have a video camera, switch it on and look through the view finder. Let it roll.

• If it's a person, look at them and pause it. Change something about them. Give them a different hair style, make it as ridiculous as you can. Change the clothes they are wearing into something really silly.

Give them mouse ears, flamingo legs or a beak. Imagine they are speaking like Mickey Mouse, Elmer Fudd, Donald Duck, or Morgan Freeman, have fun.

• Now play the video and speed it up, they are walking so fast, their voice speeds up. Now slow it down, soooo sloooow, they're walking so slow, they're talking so slow. Ok you get the idea. Keep messing with this. Fast, slow etc. Keep repeating until the intensity, the fear or the upset recedes.

• If it's a situation like a car crash, an accident or something that happened to you. Again take out a video camera and switch it on. This helps you to disassociate as you are now an observer.

• Imagine you are videoing the situation watching yourself. At the part that upsets you most, pause the video. Think about a time when you were watching a movie on TV. You know the music increases, your heart starts to beat faster, and then a bloody commercial for loo roll comes on. Well we're making a new movie. So you've paused your movie, press play and allow some dancing hippos to cross over the image that was upsetting you. Insert some circus music, music from the Muppet Show, Benny Hill, make something up. This breaks the intensity and pattern.

• Now go back to the start. Put your video on again and start playing the scene that was upsetting you, only now we need some more music, something ridiculous. Look on you tube for ideas. The scene is coming to the point that had really upset you, then the music changes and a duck pops his head up in front of the screen, or a flamingo, a clown, or Mr. Bean gyrates across the screen to Mr. Bombastic, you get the idea.

• Each time you do this the images and feelings will lose their intensity, they will lose the power they had over you.

• Whatever it is that bothers you, try changing the details. Flip it on its head. Turn it upside down. Change it into black and white, fade it out. Your mind will run the sequence of how you think you remember it. Reverse it. Think of making a movie, cut out scenes, put the ending first or in the middle, mess around with it and bring in some hippos in pink tutus, at worst they are cute.

• You may need to do this between three to five times each time, and repeat it over a few days or weeks to change the neural pathway response. The more you practice this the better. Your mind will keep trying to replay images that can cause you fear, just don't let them. Who makes the movies? You do darling!

This next technique is about dissociating a bad feeling. If someone annoys you or leaves you with a bad feeling that you can't shake.

Return to Universe

• Identify the feeling. Is it fear, anger, anxiety, frustration etc.?

• Imagine where that feeling is lodged, i.e. chest, tummy, back, neck etc.?

• Imagine a colour for it.

• Imagine a shape / texture.

• Then imagine plonking it onto the table, packaging it up, and then firing it up into the atmosphere, it goes higher and higher into the sky, then into outer space, into the universe for recycling, for the highest greater good, then poof, it disappears! How do you feel now, a bit lighter? Good!

• At least it will give you something to smile about.

• You may have to repeat this a few times to feel its effect.

This next technique can be used to disassociate unpleasant feelings about a person or situation.

Photo Disassociation

• Imagine a person or situation that has bothered you.

• When you think about it, are you in the picture with the person or situation in your mind? Notice how you feel, how bright is the picture? Full colour? Notice how your feelings are.

• Now imagine you are looking in on you and the person or situation as if you were a bystander. You can now see you and the person from a third perspective. Notice how you feel as an observer, you'll be slightly more detached and your feelings will be less intense.

• Imagine that you take a photo. There is a frame around the picture of you and the person and situation, and the photo is in bright colour, large and up close.

• Now flip the photo. You see the back of it. Now it twirls around and around. It goes upside down. Now it's dancing on its corner edge. It moves backwards really fast, now it zooms towards you. Then it slows down, ever so slow.

• Now start pushing that photo further away from you, so that it gets smaller and smaller and the colour starts to fade out of it, until it becomes just a white rectangle in the distance and then, poof, it disappears.

• How do you feel now?

• Repeat this, as often as necessary until you feel better about the person or situation. You need to do this three to five times each time you practice. Ideally the intensity of your feelings about the issue will lessen as the photo gets smaller.

Chapter 5

Emotional Intelligence

'Nobody can hurt you without your permission'

Mahatma Gandhi

I'm going to add to this quote and say, that nobody nor any situation can hurt you without your permission. It is only your thoughts about things that can do that. As I've said previously change the way you think about it and you'll change the way you feel. This is something I learned as I developed emotional intelligence.

So what is Emotional Intelligence and how can it help us? It is the ability to recognize, understand and manage our emotions in a positive way, which can affect our behaviour and our interactions with ourselves and others. We can learn how to bring our emotions into a state of balance, so that we're not being tossed back and forth in a sea of uncertainty.

Developing our emotional intelligence can help us to communicate more effectively, become more emphatic, find positive ways to cope, overcome challenges, relieve stress, create healthier relationships, and minimize conflicts, which can lead to a more fulfilling life.

Becoming aware of our emotions, in each moment, can help us to remain calm and focused in unsettling situations and can help us to see how they influence our thoughts and actions.

As mentioned in the section about mindfulness, most of us are on auto pilot, reacting to present situations, based on experiences we had in the past. If we centre ourselves with our breath (see the part about the breathing technique) we can come into the present moment and ask ourselves if this is the appropriate reaction right now, or are we just replaying a script we have been using all our lives.

Say for example you send a text message, and the person doesn't reply. You might think they are ignoring you. By the end of the day if they don't get in touch, you might not be in the best of moods. This could end up in a conflict. You've allowed an unanswered text to affect your mood and possibly hurt you.

From an emotional intelligence perspective, you notice that the text hasn't been answered and you consider what might be the reason, a) maybe they are too busy right now, and don't have enough time to text properly, b) maybe they don't have credit, c) maybe they are upset with you or just need some space to think, d) maybe they are a narcissist or an asshole... If you suspect the answer is d) get the feck away from them as soon as possible, it doesn't get better believe me. Leave while you have some sense of self- worth intact!

Breathe slowly and ask yourself why you feel ignored or abandoned etc. Consider all the options and wait until you hear from them before jumping to conclusions. Distract yourself with something else. What I learned from my experiences was never to assume that

I knew why someone didn't answer a text for example. It was better to wait and see if they did reply. It was wiser to become interested in an observational way, as in 'I wonder how come they haven't replied' rather than going in for the thoughts that reinforced my low self-worth, or my fears of betrayal, abandonment and so on.

I learned that if someone values you that they will reply eventually, so that they are not misunderstood. Those kind of people won't want any kind of misunderstanding between you. Generally in those instances I would text and if didn't get a reply would maybe text later or the next day, depending on the circumstances to check if they were ok, and if I didn't hear back after that I would leave it.

I only want to communicate with mutually interested people. If people want you in their life they'll make an effort to keep you. I learned how not to be needy and how not to chase people. I read a book called the Four Agreements by Don Miguel Ruiz, and one of the agreements is 'Don't take anything personally'. This is powerful. You are more empowered when you develop emotional intelligence. Here's some ways to practice it.

• Calm down, take time out regularly to breathe slowly and practice observing how you feel in each situation, so that you can respond in a conscious manner based on this moment rather than your experience from the past.

• Learn to trust your emotions and how you feel, be true to yourself, and you'll suffer less.

• Notice your behaviour at different times, and take full responsibility for how you choose to feel and respond, no one can make you angry, frustrated or sad, that's a choice you make. Name the emotion and distance yourself from it. Say 'I am experiencing anger, frustration or sadness'. There is a message for us in every emotion. Usually it's because an expectation of ours or a need hasn't been met or we've experienced something we can't fully control.

• Be proactive instead of reactive. Try and see a few different possible perspectives to any situation.

• Ask questions: What is important now? What am I learning from this? Do I need to set healthier boundaries? Are my needs being met? What are the consequences if I say or do this? Are my expectations realistic?

Releasing Trapped Emotions

I've mentioned 'The Emotion Code' by Dr Bradley Nelson more than a few times, so I think it only fair that I share more about it now.

I was having great difficulty with my left foot. It started with pain in my two smallest toes and then spread to the ball of my foot. It was gradually getting more and more painful, and I was finding it hard to walk on it. I love my daily walk so this was distressing me.

I had relapsed on my healthy eating plan and was eating more sugars, so I cut them down, but it didn't work. I knew the left side of my body represented my past, so I knew there was a clue there. Some things had happened to me which I had very little control over and they were still upsetting me, even though I was trying to accept the lessons and practicing all that I teach. I am human. My body was still giving me a message that we had some work to do, but I was at a loss as to what that might be. I had tried everything I knew.

I went to a podiatrist to see if they could help. Unfortunately the foot manipulations felt like something out of the torture chambers of the Inquisition. I went a few times and realized it was hurting me more. I was also told that one leg was longer than the other, I'd never heard that said to me before.

One evening after a particularly grueling session, I sat down to watch Gaia.com, a spiritual version of Netflix. Up popped a suggestion of a documentary called E-Motion, so I watched it. There were a lot of people talking about the link between emotions and pain. The Emotion Code book was mentioned.

I ordered the book the next day and it arrived within a few days. I began to devour the information rapidly. I was fascinated to learn all about trapped emotions and how releasing them could clear blocks, release pain and many things besides. The book held nothing back, it even included charts and techniques, so that the reader could begin right then and there.

I was fascinated when I came across a part that mentioned a client that Dr Bradley Nelson had, and that he'd noticed the client had one leg longer than the other. And that when he silently observed an area of the clients' body and checked again, that his legs were the same length when he looked away from the area, but that when the he looked again at the same area his legs were different lengths again. I used the sway test to get yes or no answers from my body, I realized then that my body was saying no to the treatment I was receiving.

I didn't go back to the podiatrist, but I did practice The Emotion Code, and my foot did get better pretty quickly. I had a lot of trapped emotions that were lodging in my left foot. Everyone has a weak area where emotions and their energy can get trapped.

Like in nature, we humans gravitate towards things that are good for us and are repelled by those things that are not good for us. Unfortunately we let our needs and wants interfere. The Emotion Code teaches us muscle testing to get a yes or a no answer from our bodies, very like kinesiology.

There is a system of meridians throughout the body that can trap emotions, from this lifetime, from ancestors and past lives. By using a certain magnet or by using your hand with intention you can clear these energetic patterns.

We can also absorb emotions from other people and from the earth. I think there is a very great intelligence in existence that has us all connected to each other.

And no I don't fully understand the workings of all this. I asked my body, using the sway test to get yes or no answers, if there was a way of not absorbing emotions from others and I got a no. There must be a higher reason to all this. A great wisdom. But the problem is, if we don't know about this, it can cause us pain and suffering. About 90 % of what is wrong, doesn't even belong to us. I know this from clearing myself and others. Initially I had a lot of stuff that was mine, but as time goes on, it's mostly from others.

If I'm feeling a bit off and I can't figure out what caused it, I do a clearing on myself. I always feel lighter and better afterwards.

I've done some great work on myself, friends and family since I got the book, and I highly recommend you check it out yourself. There's a lot to it. It's a great way of releasing emotional baggage. However I must add that after releasing trapped emotions, which are energy, if you or someone you've cleared, persists in repeating the same thoughts and emotional patterns, then you're going to re trap that same energy, and you won't change anything.

116

PAULA O'SULLIVAN
The Happiness Ratio

'At any moment, you have a choice that leads you closer to your spirit or further away from it. Letting go, gives us freedom, and freedom is the only condition for happiness, if in our heart, we still cling to anything – anger, anxiety, or possessions, we cannot be free'

Thich Nhat Hanh

There have been many researchers claiming to have found a mathematical formula for finding happiness. Some said the ratio was three positives to every one negative, and others claimed that the ratio was five positives to one negative, in order to be happy and flourish. But how can anyone really measure such a thing? We are all responding to things in our own unique way, based on our individual experiences. I think it takes a bit more than this to find it.

In the past, in times of crises, when I was feeling low and overwhelmed, it was very difficult to find any positives. When we're feeling low, we have a distorted perception of things, we have an all or nothing mind set and everything seems to be going wrong, and knowing about the ratio doesn't necessarily help to make it any better.

However as I practiced becoming aware of my thoughts and by developing my emotional intelligence, I discovered that I could change my perception. That as I changed my thoughts about things, the things I thought about changed, in a way. I saw that a situation was just a situation, I could think about it in many ways, which could affect how I felt about it. I could be either miserable or happy the amount of effort involved was pretty much the same. I found that I could be happy even if I didn't have everything that I wanted.

I found that by cultivating an attitude of gratitude in everything, that I was able to tip the balance. I was able to become happy regardless of what happened, most of the time. Suddenly my awareness was focused on all that was going right in my life, even though it could easily have seemed like a shambles. I would shift my focus again and again each time. I would just keep asking myself, 'Tell me one thing that's going right… great now another… now another' Then my mind would switch back to focus on all that was missing, that it thought I needed to be happy.

So I would shift my focus back to all that I did have, even though at times it wasn't as I wanted it to be. I've been lucky enough to always have clothes to wear, to have a roof over my head, some money, no matter how meagre and some food to eat. So by viewing it from that perspective, I was luckier than some. I could be grateful about that. Then I would start seeking out what each experience was teaching me, looking to find where the positive lesson was in it all. I became quite the philosopher!

And like the quote at the start says, we have a choice in any moment to move closer to our spirit or away from it. Your spirit sees life as an adventure with different opportunities to learn and grow from your experiences.

It is our attachment through our thoughts about things that keeps us from finding happiness. You can find happiness right now, this moment if you wish, by just enveloping yourself in gratitude for all that you do have right now, it turns everything into more than enough. And yes the personality will always want something more, will always want things to be different right now, but you get to choose what you want to put your focus on, and if those things make you feel good, you will have found your happiness ratio. Or you can just practice finding three or five positive things or even ten or twenty!

Interdependence

Most of us interact in only two ways in our relationships, either through a state of dependence or independence. We have not learnt that everything we seek is inside of us already. We are not aware of our inner power. We seek happiness outside of ourselves, in relationships, or in the accumulation of material possessions etc.

Dependence on others or things to completely satisfy our needs can leave us very vulnerable, as our expectations invariably won't get met a lot of the time. Independence means we don't really seek out the help of others, we become kind of disconnected from each other, as we strive to meet our own needs only. But there is another way of being, it's called interdependence.

Let's compare the three ways of being in relationships.

Interdependence is a way of being and acting that takes into account your needs and at the same time cares about others' needs.

Dependence is needing someone else to take care of you, to fix you, to support you, to do things for you, to fulfil your needs, in ways that you either can't do for yourself, or haven't learned the skills, it can be a form of helplessness.

Independence is, in a way, ignoring others and our coexistence, it's about wanting to deal with everything on your own, and in your own way and not acknowledge a need for support.

With *Interdependence*, we strive for balance in all our interactions. We aim for 'win /win', i.e. both parties have their say, both parties get their needs met without compromise, or it's a 'no deal'. If we make a sacrifice, then the other party will also make one to balance the arrangement. With dependence and independence, most of us don't really listen, we base what we hear from others on our own autobiographical experiences.

With interdependence we seek first to really understand the wants and needs of others, before we try to be understood ourselves. We begin the dance of creative cooperation between each other. We begin to value our differences and respect each other's uniqueness. We aim not to blame when things don't work out, but seek instead to examine, the causes and effects of all behaviours involved, with each party accepting full responsibility for the part they have played.

Being interdependent with others becomes a balanced energy exchange, with neither party draining the other. Each stays true to their selves, and become involved without the demand that either should sacrifice their values or integrity. It paves the way for open communication and honesty. It creates a safe environment where both parties can become aware of their needs. We realize that we can't change anyone, we can only change our behaviour, so we treat others as we'd like to be treated, and we won't tolerate for long, not being treated with respect.

We begin to view ourselves as already whole, balanced and complete, there is nothing to gain from anyone. Our interactions become a mutual giving, to enhance, not to fill a void. We create and maintain healthy boundaries, knowing how to give help, but also knowing when to protect our own energy and health by saying no.

Something worthy of striving for? Make up your own mind.

The Relationship Bank

I wish I'd been aware of the concept of a relationship bank account in my early years of relationships, it would have saved everyone concerned so much pain.

It was after reading Steven Covey's book, 'The Seven Habits of Highly Effective People' that I raised my awareness. I had been accused on many occasions over the years of 'keeping score', but in all honesty, I could see that things weren't balanced. I was giving way more in my relationships and feeling more than a tad resentful. But there isn't any blame in my mind now, I see that I didn't have the confidence or the sense of worthiness to actually ask for what I wanted. I was caught up in my childhood conditioning of how I thought things were meant to be, based on the ways I saw relationships playing out around me.

Healthy relationships aim to meet each other's needs. If you consider the concept of 'Evolve or Die', all things must continue to grow, or they die. Ideas evolve or grow into plans and actions, or else they die as unfulfilled wishes. In the same way, relationships and friendships evolve with the building of trust, honesty, communication, clear expectations, integrity, little kindnesses, courtesies, and sincerity.

A healthy relationship is about giving and receiving. If we don't have these little things, we can develop anger, resentment, bitterness, mistrust and conflict. We must put more deposits into the relationship bank to enable it to flourish, and aim to make less withdrawals. If you're wondering why you would bother, then ask yourself why you are staying in that relationship to begin with.

So how do we make a deposit? How do we make our relationships better and happier? How do we evolve?

Understanding

It's really essential that we try to understand the other person's point of view. Most of us are trying to get our view understood first. We are all reacting based on our own experiences, which may be different from another person's. If we ask questions to find out how the other person feels, we will maybe understand their perspective and perhaps see how our actions may or may not have contributed.

Most of us have a basic need to be listened to, to feel that what we are expressing is valid. You'll make a serious withdrawal if you invalidate what someone says they are feeling, because it's real for them. Sometimes we have subconscious scripts playing in our minds based on how unworthy we feel etc. and this can colour our perceptions, but if you want your relationship to blossom, it's worth taking the time to listen to each other and try to understand where they might be coming from.

Expectations

Most of our thoughts and feelings of hurt and frustration happen when someone's behaviour doesn't meet our expectations. The most difficult thing for most of us, is to actually ask the other person what they expect from us, and to tell them what we expect from them. We prefer to mind read instead – it's much less confrontational – there's much less chance of being rejected! But this can drive you bat shit crazy, because you start making up a lot of stories in your head, which may not be the full truth of the situation at all! When expectations aren't met, people fall out, become distant, argue a lot and sometimes have affairs and or leave.

Here's a rather open minded question based on a perspective I reached from my own personal experiences with this. If you're not meeting someone's needs and they have an affair, who's cheating who? Just something to ponder on.

Keeping your promises

Do what you say you will do. Say what you mean, and mean what you say, if you want to keep a healthy relationship balance. This will build trust, and trust is hugely important. It's also imperative that you keep your promises to yourself also, otherwise you'll probably spend the rest of your life mentally beating yourself up, and meta-physically you'll start attracting those people who will emotionally abuse you. I know, because this is what happened to me, until I changed things.

Appreciation

Mutual appreciation, admiration and gratitude are real relationship builders. It's the little daily genuine compliments, concern, kind-nesses, courtesies, the wanting the very best for the other, that creates a healthy relationship balance.

Honesty

Admit and apologize sincerely when you fuck up. We all do it at some stage, we're busy, we're careless, we have our pride, we don't ask for what we want. If you break the trust you have between you, it's like smashing a plate and gluing it back together. The cracks will still be there, you've weakened your relationship, and you've made a withdrawal. If you were depositing regularly your relationship might survive this, if you weren't, it may not.

Chapter 6

Meeting Your Un-met Needs

'We're only as needy, as our unmet needs'

John Bowlby

Identifying the difference between our needs and our wants, can be the beginning of a very beautiful friendship, with ourselves and others.

Most of us have some very basic common needs, including the need to be loved, accepted, respected, touched, seen, connected, and heard, to feel safe and to feel special.

What happens to us if these basic needs have not been met, either in our early childhood experiences or later on as life progresses?

Well, we'll go looking to get them met. Everyone you meet, is trying to get their needs met, in some way, shape or form. Knowing this can help us to understand others better. But what about ourselves?

If we don't know exactly what our needs are, then we might get addicted to something, or find ourselves repeatedly experiencing relationships or situations that cause us deeper pain, in an attempt to cover up our distress or unease.

We'll feel we need to have 'something' in our lives to compensate for the loss we feel inside, at not getting our needs met. This can also trigger a deep depression, disconnection and feelings of abandonment and un-worthiness.

And there's no guarantee that even if you can identify your needs, that someone or something else will actually satisfy that for you. It's a huge burden to put on someone to expect them to meet all your needs. And even with alcohol, drugs, sex, pornography etc. You'll still feel the void after the bottle is empty, the high has subsided, the sex is over, the movies or pictures cease to stimulate you. You'll have to constantly 'Chase the Dragon', as they say, for your next high. And in between those highs, it can get very low indeed.

If you don't find out what you really want, and learn to ask for it in a healthy way, you'll end up attracting others who also share some similar unmet needs. Yes I know, you're probably thinking, now wouldn't that be nice, but I can tell you, it can get real dysfunctional!

What's the difference between a need and a want then?

A 'Need' is something you feel you have to have (or you'll die)

A 'Want' is something you would like to have (you won't die if you don't get it)

Psychologically, not feeling loved, can make us die a little inside. In some cases where babies weren't touched or stroked in the early days, they actually died. Those that didn't die, grew up pre- disposed to depression, anxiety, violence, addictions etc. and were averse to feeling love or being touched. (Psychology experts will tell you that if you didn't bond with someone in childhood, that you won't be able to bond with anyone later on, but you can change this, it wasn't easy, but I did!) So in a way these things are needs for our healthy functioning, and for our soul too.

But what if, in all the searching, what if in all the wrong relationships, you still didn't meet anyone who really loved you, cared for you, heard you etc.? What then?

Like I said, most people find ways to cope, to compensate, and that's ok, we're all doing the best we can to keep surviving, but if all this is causing you mental and emotional pain, I'd like to tell you, it doesn't have to be that way.

We cannot change anything until we become aware of it. So we need to ask ourselves what do we want, and what do we need, for to create a healthy balance in our lives? And then we need to find the courage to begin asking for that.

More importantly though, because as I said you may not get what you ask for, is to learn how to meet some of your own needs.

No this isn't an easy task, there's no quick fix, it's a process, which needs to be practiced and tested out over periods of time.

You may have to explore issues like your self- esteem, your core beliefs or being addicted among others.

In my early childhood, I didn't feel loved, accepted, respected, heard, touched, seen or connected. I had very low self- esteem and a general feeling of unworthiness. This affected my whole life up until I was 44! It affected my career choices and my relationships.

The need to be loved kept me tied to many mental, emotional and physically abusive situations. I survived them, but my soul suffered from all of this. I never found love in those relationships. I found sex, which I thought was love, but it wasn't, and it certainly wasn't a good enough reason for me to stay so long with those experiences, but hey, that's what expecting others to meet your unmet needs can do for you.

Then I took my first steps on an amazing journey into meeting my own needs, and that has changed everything for me.

It started with learning to actually LOVE MYSELF. That meant dealing with the negative Self Talk. I realized that I just wanted people to be nice to me, because I'm actually a nice person, and more importantly, I needed ME to be nice to ME!

Once this process started, I began to ask myself better questions.

• If I loved myself, what would be different?

How would I talk to myself if I loved myself? What kind of friends or relationships would I tolerate if I loved myself? I've distanced myself from people who are just plain unaware, if they're not honouring and respecting themselves, they are not going to be able to honour and respect me. If they are destroying themselves, they're not going to be in a position to celebrate my blossoming, now are they? People who are stuck will keep you stuck and retard your positive growth.

• What way would I treat my body if I loved myself? I stopped drinking alcohol, I choose my foods more carefully, I rest when I need to rest, I meditate and exercise daily. If no one wanted to listen to me, how could I get my voice or thoughts heard? I started to journal, then blog, then that turned into a book, now I've several books in the making, there's always someone out there who might be interested in what you've learnt.

• How could I meet my own sexual needs in a safe way? (Ha, ha, use your imagination for that one!) How could I experience touch? I got massages and Reiki and began to feel more comfortable with hugging, free hug anyone?

• How could I feel more connected? Spiritual practices of meditation, mindfulness and reading inspirational books, helped me see that I am already connected to everything, it was only my thoughts and feelings that made me think otherwise.

• How could I feel seen? I started making motivational videos! I started to put myself out there to help people also.

• How could I feel respected? Once I started to respect myself, I found I attracted more people who did respect me, and could easily distance myself from those who don't, what they think of me doesn't matter, I know my worth now !

• How could I feel safe? By not allowing my needs or my wants to get me into potentially dangerous situations, which they did in the past!

This began the most loving relationship I've ever had! I'm 100% there for me. I buy myself flowers and gifts. I don't criticize myself anymore, I know I'm doing the best I can in any moment. I do review my performance at the end of each day, I do seek to improve myself as I deem necessary. I'm in the process of honouring my higher ideals and I love, accept and respect myself, enough to walk away from anyone or anything that is not honouring my higher ideals.

This hasn't been easy, because I'm human, and I keep getting tested, I'm not fully there yet, I'm not even sure there is a 'there' to get to, but hey I'm in a process ! I've identified my essential needs, and I've also divided some of those into wants. I'm not needy now. I won't accept any old kind of relationship anymore. I might want intimacy, and companionship but I'm happy with myself, I don't need it, there's a difference, I can be more choosy now. There's great freedom in that!

Addicted

'I have absolutely no pleasure in the stimulants in which I sometimes so madly indulge. It has not been in the pursuit of pleasure that I have periled life and reputation and reason. It has been the desperate attempt to escape from torturing memories, from a sense of insupportable loneliness and a dread of some strange impending doom'

Edgar Allan Poe

Whatever you may be addicted to, in order to be free, you'll need to find out what your addiction appears to be giving you. We won't give something up unless there is the promise of a better life waiting for us. Every behaviour has a payback, we get something out of it, or we wouldn't do it. We are motivated in two basic ways: by the 'Promise of Pleasure' or the 'Fear of Pain'.

When we are addicted to something, it can appear that this helps us to deal with our needs and desires, but usually it's just a quick fix, a band aid solution. This is why people remain addicted for so long. The effects of the alcohol or drugs wear off and we are painfully aware of our reality once again, the adrenalin kick from gambling or sex wears off, and we have to re- experience it again to feel good, hopeful or less lonely.

The stressful situations keep happening and we have to keep smoking to help us 'cope'.

You think the addiction is helping you to cope, but it's not really solving the issue for you, it's actually creating more problems. Unless you focus on the benefits of quitting the addiction, and begin to imagine how good that will feel, and how your life and relationships will improve in so many ways, you will remain stuck.

Most of us find it difficult to imagine what we DO want. Mostly we focus on what we DON'T want to happen. This is the fear of pain again, which stops us from moving forward.

When we're addicted, we have given up our own power. We are saying to the thing or person 'Save me, I am powerless without you'.

Most of us who are or have been addicted to something, have very deep emotional needs that weren't or aren't being met in a healthy way. This is not so easy to address, so we reach out for something to make it all better, but the pain is still there at the end of the bottle, cigarette, drug, gambling slip, one night stand or whatever. The story is and will remain the same, unless you decide now to change the ending.

Remember that no matter what has happened to you in your life, you still have a choice how to think about it. You can be a strong survivor, or a helpless victim of your circumstances. As I keep repeating, most of us just want to feel loved, accepted, and respected. If we are expecting the world to meet our basic needs, we may be disappointed.

This creates havoc within us, we feel we aren't good enough, and we become our own destroyers. We have to find a way to love, accept and respect ourselves first and to discover our own power, regardless of others, then we can be free.

131

Tips & Techniques for Quitting Smoking

You can adjust this for most things that you want to quit, just edit it to make it more relevant. So you've decided to quit smoking? Maybe this is your first real attempt to quit, or maybe you've tried everything you can think of and haven't succeeded so far.

Well I'd like to share a few things that might help you to succeed once and for all. Remember we only fail when we stop trying. Although 'Yoda' from 'Star Wars' tells us, to 'do or do not, there is no try'. In a way trying actually gives us an excuse to fail. 'Look I've tried everything and it hasn't worked, I'm never going to quit etc.'… well it doesn't have to be that way.

Begin with being very honest with yourself, yes yourself! Forget about what everyone else in your life wants or thinks about you smoking. Do YOU really want to quit, for your OWN personal reasons? On a scale of 1 to 10 with 10 being very committed, where are you? If you are under a 6, you just haven't put enough focus on this issue, let's see if I can help you change that. If you want to that is!

Get a sheet of paper, it's time to make a plan.

First, in order to change anything in your life, you need to know what the habit of smoking actually gives you. Every behaviour has some form of payback, otherwise you wouldn't do it. We are primarily motivated in two ways, by the promise of pleasure or the fear of pain. Your promise of pleasure mostly wins out, although the fear of the pain of something can also be a strong motivator which could stop you from even trying to quit.

Ok so you have a piece of paper? Draw a line dividing the page in half. On the left side, write the title: **Reasons why I smoke**. And on the right hand side of the page, write the title: **Benefits from quitting**. Now list all those things, the Reasons may be 1.Relaxation, 2. Dealing with stress, 3.Clears my mind and helps me think clearly and 4. Social inclusion the Benefits may include better health, more money, clothes smell cleaner, feel empowered and a sense of achievement, food tastes nicer etc.

Be very honest with yourself. Money will not be a benefit, if you are already financially well off, unless you decide on something to spend that extra money on.

Now you have an idea of what smoking is giving you, and what would be the benefits of quitting.

Let's see if we can balance some of the reasons, with some techniques. Ok if you have reasons like, 1, 2 & 3, think about this. What are you actually doing when you smoke?

Reasons why I smoke	Benefits from quitting
Relaxation	Better health, I will feel fitter
Dealing with stress	More money
Clears my mind and helps me	Clothes smell cleaner
think clearly	Feel empowered and a sense of
Social inclusion etc.	achievement
	Food tastes nicer
	More energy
	Better relationships etc.

You are breathing in very slowly and deeply, and you are breathing out very slowly and deeply.

When we are 'stressed out' or need to relax, it is because we have triggered the 'Stress Response' in our body. If you think of it like this: Your body and mind is like a very busy building site with lots of workers rushing around doing many jobs. When you are stressed, a signal travels up to the brain area and puts these workers on high alert.

Oxygen gets pumped immediately from your brain down into your heart and lungs, so that you can't think clearly, it puts you into survival mode. Cortisol and adrenalin gets pumped in excess. This all allows you to have the strength to fight or flee from whatever is distressing you. Ha! But most of us can't fight or run away. So we grab an oul smoke to help us, but what are we really doing? We are breathing! Yes we are breathing in deeply, yes it's got a lethal concoction of chemicals in it, but we are breathing in and out deeply. Why? Because the only way to reverse the stress response is to breathe deeply!

Now that you know that, here is the breathing technique again, which, if you really want to quit, will give you everything that, reasons for smoking 1, 2 & 3 gave you, except the chemicals!

Breathing Technique

Find a quiet place initially, where you won't be disturbed, lock yourself in the loo if you have too!

Close your eyes, uncross your arms and legs. Now breathe in very slowly and deeply. To help you with this, imagine that the breath is travelling up from your fingertips, all the way up your arms, to your head, chest and belly on the in breath, and out and down through your body, down through your legs, feet and toes on the out breath. Do this slowly at least 5 times.

* * *

Now doing this sends the signal to all those hard workers in your body to go take a tea break! They can relax and do what they normally do!

You will now feel calmer and more relaxed and your mind will be clearer. But wait, we're not done yet. We still have to deal with your thoughts. It is your thoughts and beliefs about things that are keeping you stuck in the habit of smoking. A belief is a thought you keep thinking over and over.

Every time you think a thought it strengthens a neural pathway in the brain, this becomes a belief, which then forms a habit, and will then affect how you behave. This will in time become your unquestioning automatic response to things in life.

How do we change this? Use the breathing technique on a regular daily basis, for example every morning and evening and during the day, when stuck in traffic, a queue, or when being challenged by life, then you'll have enough oxygen to be able to reason this out more effectively.

Then remember this there are …

TWO ways of thinking about things

The Worst Way: Focuses on all that is going wrong or may go wrong, you play movies in your mind about not being able to cope with quitting, you feel all the dreadful feelings of failure etc. You can't see yourself doing it. In the battle between imagination and reality, imagination will always win, so as long as your focus is on the pain or the fear, then that is all you will see and experience.

The Best Way: Focuses on all that could go right, you play movies in your mind about all the ways quitting smoking can benefit you. You see yourself using the breathing technique, you see yourself choosing a different way to think. You imagine how wonderful it is to be finally free of this habit. You see and feel the excitement, the empowerment of achieving something in your life. You use your imagination to focus on the pleasure of being free of smoking. In your mind you play out your daily routines and plan what will be different now that you are a non- smoker.

Now you have two things to try, a breathing technique and the choice of how to think about this, but there is one more thing that will help you. The mind movies that you play in your mind and the feelings they conjure up, will either keep you stuck or will help to liberate you.

Remember a RUT is only a Record of Unhelpful Thoughts. Stay out of a RUT, by choosing the best way of thinking. Talk back to any thoughts that tell you to give in.

Use a journey statement to help you, one like:

'As I become and stay a non-smoker, my life improves in many ways,' or write your own one that resonates with you.

As you change your thoughts, you will change how you feel. Don't believe me? Close your eyes, think of something sad, go on bring it all up. Open your eyes, feel really good do you? No? Ok close your eyes again, think of something that made you happy, go on bring it all up, that lovely feeling in your chest, or tummy. Open your eyes, feel really good do you?

Now here's the mind movie again for you. Find a quiet time when you won't be disturbed. Close your eyes and breathe in and out slowly, so that you can think clearly.

Mind Movie

Use your imagination to imagine that you are walking into your own private movie theatre.

You are perfectly safe in here and you choose a seat. You look up at the screen and see a scene from your life on pause.

Think about how you DO want to be in this scene. Not how you 'don't want to be' (that's the worst way of thinking!) Now think about how you want to be as a non-smoker. What will you be wearing, what will you look like, what will you feel like? See, hear, feel, and imagine your life as a non-smoker. How wonderful does it feel to have achieved this? Imagine yourself doing all you can to make sure that you remain a non-smoker. What kind of things are you telling yourself? What kind of scenes are you imagining for yourself?

Press play and let the movie unfold as you would want it to be, take your time with this. Now press pause, re think what you could improve on, then rewind it back very fast and press play, imagining any changes you want to make, take your time. Press pause, review if there is anything you can improve on, then play again and so on, do this at least three times or more, regularly. It is no different to what we already do, except that we usually play disaster movies instead.

If you can see yourself doing it, then you are already halfway there. The next thing you do when you have a clear idea of what you want your experience to be like, is to put into action all the techniques that feel right for you.

Now finally plan out your first week as a non-smoker. Get rid of the spare cigarettes, roll ups, cigars etc. Yes even the little glass box on the wall, with the break in case of emergency! If you decide to do this right there won't be a need for it!

Break the habit easily by slightly changing your routine. If you have a smoke with a cuppa in a certain cup every morning, change the cup for the first week, so that you break the habit association with the thing you smoke. Ever hear a song, or smell a scent that brings back a memory? Well it might be the same with letting go of smoking. Be prepared. If you smoke before you shower, change the routine and shower first, then do something else where the cigarette would be, read, or go for a walk, or use the breathing techniques etc. Plan out your day and be prepared.

Use your breathing technique.

Challenge your thoughts and change your focus to what you do want.

Play your Mind Movie in your imagination.

If you want it badly enough, you'll make it happen, if not, you'll just make an excuse. The choice is yours

Chapter 7

Mastering the Self

'Self-Mastery and the consistent care of one's mind, body and soul, are essential to finding one's higher self, and living the life of one's dreams'

Robin Sharma

As within, so without, to thine own self be true. Self- Mastery means learning self-control. It means learning how to control our thoughts and our emotions. It means being the same in all situations and having a core of stability within. We are only as strong as our greatest weakness, don't worry, life will test you on this!

Most of us are like chameleons, we are constantly changing in response to what is happening to us, without consistency. Self-mastery gives us a choice, it helps us to be more in control of ourselves. And no it doesn't give us a license to control others. Ask yourself this: If I'm not in control of my thoughts and emotions, then who is? You don't have to be a victim, you can choose to be a survivor instead.

Most of us have been conditioned to focus on altering the externals in our lives. We wait for everyone else and everything to change first. This makes for a very frustrating life journey!

When we change, we will find that things change around us. 'Nothing happens until something moves' (Einstein)

You're probably asking the question 'Why do I have to be the first to make a move or change?' I'll answer you with this question. 'How's that going for you so far?' If you're happy with your results, carry on as you are.

Well for me anyway it didn't bring me to anywhere worth going. It was with beginning the process of learning self-mastery that my life began to change in many happier ways. I'm not saying I'm there yet. Life has many lessons and challenges for me that always keep me on my toes. I'm a work in progress, I'm further on than I was, and I'm getting there, as they say.

Ok so how do you begin this process?

Awareness

Start observing yourself in various situations. Are you doing or saying what you want to do and say, or is there some kind of an agenda to be met? Are you looking for approval? Is it meeting an unmet need? Are you doing and saying things to just fit in with the general crowd, or are you being true to yourself? Watch your reactions. Watch any self-talk. Become aware of the two ways of thinking that I mentioned earlier.

As we master ourselves, we begin to notice all these things, and with the observation comes the choice in how we really want to be.

Identify Your Needs Versus Your Wants

This is really important. Most of us are on auto pilot (not fully aware) we all have basic needs, including security, sex, love and belonging, financial, freedom, fun etc. True needs take into account the higher greater good and serve our soul. Our wants can override this and serve our ego or lower selves, they can lead us into selfishness and a desire to satisfy our own personal interests without concern for how it affects others. There's an element of developing integrity with self-mastery.

Delay Gratification

Start practicing to strengthen your will by testing yourself in small ways. Delay gratification in some area of your life regularly. Watch your wants, watch the impulses, they can be so strong.

For example: I want that biscuit, the drug, the high, the sexual release, the escape etc. but I'm consciously deciding that I'm not going to have that right now. I may wait until later, or I may defer it until tomorrow, or some other time, but now in this moment, when I'm aware, I can choose to delay, if I want to.

Observe your thoughts and feelings when you do this. Or another example: I want to say this to this person, but I'm going stay quiet instead. I'm choosing to be fully present with this person, without being compelled to make the snide remark, or say the things that could destroy the relationship, the trust etc. And yes sometimes we do have to speak up, but play with this to strengthen you will. You may decide to speak up in another moment instead.

Practice doing things you'd rather not do right now, like take out the bins, do the dishes, laundry, paperwork etc. I use a mental symbol of a foot kicking me in the ass, and saying Just Do It! I always have my sense of humour with me, it comes in handy! Notice how much energy we take up in resisting doing things. Your ego will protest, and cause a fuss, but observe it. Practice with little things, and you'll see where you can be free of external control.

Keep Your Promises

As I mentioned in a previous section. Do what you say you will do. How many times have you said you'd do something and didn't? How did you feel? Say what you mean and mean what you say. You will learn to trust yourself, and others will learn to trust you also. Practice keeping your promises to yourself and others. It starts with the little things.

Practice Being Consistent

I mentioned earlier that we are like chameleons, we are not the same people all the time. If someone is mean to us, we are mean to them, or if we're afraid, we'll be mean behind their backs instead. If life throws us a curve ball, we disintegrate, however momentarily. We're constantly being driven this way and that by relentless challenges. Our self-esteem plays a huge part in this too, and the more you develop a balanced self-esteem, the more you can be consistent with anything that happens. It gives you a strong core of stability and you will be the same you in all situations

Being Proactive

'Do what you can, with what you have, where you are'

Theodore Roosevelt

There were times in my life when I couldn't get started to change anything, I was suffering from 'Perfectionism'. I was waiting for everything to be perfect before I could begin. I could see what needed to change, but I couldn't imagine the steps to get there, I didn't feel it was the right time, I didn't have enough money, the confidence or the right education. It all seemed so overwhelming and impossible, so I would just keep doing what I was doing, over and over again, hoping that something would change. But of course nothing ever did, because how can we expect to get a different result from doing the same old things? We can't!

I've said already that in order to change anything, we must first become aware of where we are, and where we'd like to be and accept the reality. Then we need to make a plan. A plan is like an oar in a boat, it will help direct you where you want to go. Most of us are like boats without oars, allowing life's circumstances to direct us all over the place. 'Between stimulus and response, man has the freedom to choose' Victor Frankl quote. And we can choose where we want to go in life and how we want to respond to what is happening.

We can act or be acted upon. An example of this was, I found myself in financial difficulty, unable to pay the full mortgage. I could have put my head in the sand and ignored the problem. I would then have been acted upon. Every action or inaction on our behalf has a consequence. I chose to be proactive and approached the bank, yes several times, but I just wouldn't give up. While I was waiting for them to engage with me, I decided to pay the small amount that I could afford, weekly into my account regardless. I did this for two years, and finally they did come back to me and we came to an arrangement.

We sit around waiting for the magic wand to appear and solve all our problems, which rarely happens. We are a part of the problem and a part of the solution. When I wasn't earning enough, I started making and selling my jewellery, artwork, writing, my photography and I set up a monthly craft market. Some things didn't work out as planned, but I kept asking, 'what else can I do?'

We need to become aware of the things we can have some control over and focus more on that area, than those that we can't.

So, what can you do, right now, where you are, with what you have? If you're in debt, approach the lenders, agree a small amount with each. If you're in relationship difficulties, talk to the person involved and discuss each other's needs.

If you're living in Ireland and looking for a job, consider retraining, look at www.skillnets.ie/unemployed, or www.alison.com, there are hundreds of free courses. Or your country may have similar available, just do a search.

Make a plan, set a goal, decide where you want to go, or you'll just drift to any old place. All things are created twice, first in the mind, and then in your reality. Make sure you're getting the results that you really want to get!

Living with Intention

'Such a simple concept, yet so true, that which we manifest is before us, we are the creators of our own destiny. Be it through intention or ignorance, our successes and our failures, have been brought on by none other than ourselves'

Garth Stein

As a person who in the past liked to blame everything for the way my life wasn't working out, the overwhelming sense of responsibility I felt, when I discovered that I was actually creating my reality (even if it was mostly unconsciously) hit me like a whack to the side of the head!

I became aware of how we can sabotage our lives either consciously or unconsciously. I found that when we are aligned with the Divine Design, our Destiny, we know it in our hearts, and we feel really happy inside, there is no mental conflict.

By learning to live with intention, we can create the kind of story of our lives that we do want to be telling. There are some basic universal principals that are little known, and these are very important if you want to begin to express the Divine idea in your life.

One of them is 'As within, so without': as within in your mind and your subconscious mind, then so without in your reality. Look at your life right now, it is a mirror reflection of what is going on in your mind. You focus on lack and financial issues, bingo, here they come! You focus on illness and here it is! Quite distressing isn't it?

And I'm not going to be able to offer you a miracle quick fix, but if you are really eager to change this unhappy reality, quite simply change your focus of thoughts, change the words you are using, the story you are telling, and you will change the emotions you feel, and your reality will mirror back to you these different situations. Now it may take a while, I learned patience eventually! I had to!

Law of Divine Oneness: everything is connected to everything else, and we affect each other and the universe with our thoughts, beliefs and deeds.

Law of Vibration: everything in the universe moves, and vibrates in circular patterns, everything has its own vibrational frequency, including thoughts, feelings etc.

Law of Action: we must engage in actions that support what we want to manifest. If you want to receive love give love, if you want more money, give money.

Law of Correspondence: as above, so below, as above in heaven, universe, so below on earth, and also as above in your mind, imagination, thoughts, so below in your body and reality. As within, so without, your thoughts, emotions and actions are mirrored back to you by reality.

Law of Cause and Effect: every action has a consequence, so we reap what we sow.

Law of Compensation: the visible effects of our deeds or what we have sown are given to us in the forms of gifts, blessings, inheritances, friends etc. We don't always receive from the person we have given to or have been nice to, but it always comes back to us in some form or another.

Law of Attraction: thoughts, words, deeds, feelings etc. produce energies. Like attracts like energies, negative attracts negative, positive attracts positive.

Law of Perpetual Transmutation of Energy: we all have the power within to change conditions in our lives. Energies have higher or lower vibrations, by raising our energies we can transform lower energies.

Law of Relativity: everything is relative, there is always someone worse off than us. We all experience problems, or tests of initiation, if we can see these as a challenge and stay focused in the heart when solving them, we strengthen the light within us and can move closer to God Source.

Law of Polarity: everything has an opposite, we can transform undesirable thoughts by focusing on the opposite. We can transform an undesirable life by focusing on the desired life.

Law of Rhythm: everything vibrates and moves to certain rhythms, these establish cycles, seasons, stages of development, patterns etc. We can rise above negative cycles, knowing that this too shall pass.

Law of Gender: everything has its feminine (yin) and masculine (yang) principles, the basis of all creation. Passive and active, thoughts and deeds or action. Nothing happens until something moves. We strive for balance to create what we want.

There is a sentence in the Bible that refers to 'if any two of you shall agree, it shall be done'. The usual interpretation of this is, if you can get a likeminded person to be interested in your plans, then it shall manifest, which helps, but there is also another meaning, which is if you can get your subconscious and your conscious mind to agree, then it will manifest really quickly.

As I've said before, your conscious mind is like the captain of a ship giving the orders, and the subconscious is like the engine of the ship, it just follows orders. You tell it that there isn't enough, and it says ok, lets create lack! It is the genie in the bottle, it is not the reasoning mind, and it cannot tell the difference between imagination and reality, and your imagination always wins!

How do we get the two minds to agree? Well we must remove the resistance. We need to uproot the programming and patterns that aren't serving us. We can also use affirmations continuously that fire us up and that feel right. Read 'The works of Florence Scovel Shinn' I highly recommend it.

But for now I have found the following affirmation to be extremely effective. 'Infinite Spirit, open the way for the Divine Design of my life to manifest, let the genius within me now be released, let me now express the Divine idea in my mind, body and affairs, let me see clearly the perfect plan' (Florence Scovel Shinn affirmation) Words on their own are merely vain repetitions though, you must feel as though it is already here for this to work.

Create consciously!

Divided Mind – Taming the Ego

*'We must go beyond the constant clamor of ego, beyond the tools of logic and
reason, to the still, calm place within us: the realm of the soul'*

Deepak Chopra

In order to tame the ego, we must first know a little bit about it, and
why anyone would even want to tame it. Notice I said tame, and not
destroy it, as we need it in some ways to know ourselves as an individual. If you look in the dictionary, you may very well still be con-
fused as to what it is. It is described as; a person's sense of self-esteem
or self-importance, the part of the mind that mediates between the
conscious and the unconscious and is responsible for reality testing
and a sense of personal identity, and, a conscious thinking subject.
Interesting descriptions.

As mentioned before, there are many ancient stories that refer to the
beginning of the ego / divided mind, in mankind. Some relate to
Atlantis, the Annunaki, and the creator gods. There are references in
the bible too. The Adam and Eve story refers to the creation of the
Adamic and Eve race and the subsequent division of mind and the
discovery of good and evil, or more appropriately, awareness and unawareness. Apparently the original souls that came to earth, were of
a higher consciousness and were fully aware. The duality or division
of mind that ego created, led us out of paradise, not poor Eve! We're
in paradise or heaven when we're fully aware, we're in hell when we're
not!

To make it easier to understand, let's consider that Ego stands for
Edging God / or Goodness Out. If we were like the original souls,
before the fall, we would have a higher consciousness and awareness

of ourselves and others. We would make more decisions and choices based on love and compassion. We would only see the connections between souls. We would recognize the similarities we all share in this earth school.

Well the good news is, that we are like the original souls, we all have an inherent goodness in us, a light, an awareness, a conscience, or Con – Science (science of the heart)

However for a long, long time we have been conditioned to exist from the perspective of the ego.

The ego is our lower, baser self, it's all about the 'Me' part of us, and self – preservation. The higher part of ourselves, the 'I' is the soul, and is about the interconnectedness of all things.

How were we conditioned?

We've been encouraged to believe in borders, flags, nationalities, patriotism, and differences. Cautioned to ignore our intuition (tuition from within) and to be sceptic of it. The religious and political stories we've been told have separated us from ourselves and others. All arguments, all wars spring from ego, the need to be right at all costs.

We were told Eve was to blame, this started a patriarchal system that is still alive and kicking today. Women are still being treated as second class citizens around the world. Yes the men did and still do terrible things, they have been conditioned that way. Women do awful things too. In unawareness, in ego mind, we are separated from our soul's highest intentions.

We were told that the God we believe in is outside of us, and that we're not worthy enough to even gather up the crumbs from under the table of that entity. If we were encouraged to believe that entity was within each of us, we might just feel it important to respect everyone. We'd all be sacred then wouldn't we?

Far too many of us were brought up mostly in an unloving manner, with a social myth about 'sparing the rod and spoiling the child'. We now know that this way of parenting creates people who are unable to love, to connect to themselves and others. It creates people who are dependent and prone to depression, suicide and addictions. It creates people who feel they are flawed, disconnected and unworthy.

Our school systems are primarily geared towards left brained learning. Most of it is academic, analytical, rational stuff. From an early age our minds are crammed with useless shite, of little or no use in our everyday lives after we leave. We are taught to listen and repeat, and not taught to think and reason for ourselves.

We are taught to ridicule the imagination. 'It's only your imagination'- (you're just a feckin looney!)

Perhaps psychology was introduced to highlight, observe and control those individuals among us who didn't conform to left brain conditioning. If you're a right brained creative or psychic etc. you'll be seen as a weirdo, more separation. Don't worry if this depresses you, they have a pill for that!

Look around you at your world if you don't believe me for proof of ego mind in action. Poverty, hunger, greed, wars, bigotry, racism, sectarianism, pollution, slavery, crimes, mental health issues (gentle souls get depressed, in this unloving world of ego. You rarely hear of egotistical psychopaths getting depressed do you?) Pornography (this separates males and females from forming connected sacred sexual relationships) and on and on the list goes!

Is this the kind of world we want for ourselves and our children and grandchildren?

How Do we Begin to Heal the Divided Mind?

• Learn to love, accept and respect yourself, then you'll begin to love accept and respect others, you will see the connection between us all.

• Start to value your imagination. It's the greatest gift we've all been given, use it wisely and only allow what you would like to happen into it. Know that what you wish for others, you wish for yourself.

• Pay attention to your intuition and your conscience, that's your soul prompting you to other alternative more aware choices.

• If you are in two minds about some decision, ask how this will affect all concerned, if it hurts or harms another person or being, choose carefully.

• Practice using your right brain. Stories, music, art, being creative, exploring imagination etc. We need both sides of our brain, we're like an airplane flying on one wing otherwise.

• Meditate, and listen to the promptings of your higher self. There is a wiser, less mean part of us. We can be cold hearted beasts or warm hearted angels, or somewhere in between.

• Catch yourself trying to be right, trying to win at the cost of another, trying to destroy someone else, by gossiping etc. Catch yourself out.

• Find the 'I' that is observing the 'Me' Find the wiser self, watch the ego play its little games.

It's a Generational Thing

'Hurt people, hurt people. That's how pain patterns get passed on, generation after generation after generation. Break the chain today. Meet anger with sympathy, contempt with compassion and cruelty with kindness. Greet grimaces with smiles. Forgive and forget about finding fault. Love is the weapon of the future.'

Yehuda Berg

Stories in Ancient Lore suggest our thoughts, words and deeds all have the power to affect seven generations.

By the age of six, we have witnessed our parents, guardians and siblings responses to the world with all the dramas and challenges of living, and we have learned our responses from them. Unless we question it and break the pattern, this is the way we too will carry on responding and reacting for the rest of our lives. Sometimes we even end up marrying someone who is like one of our parents, so our stories continue uninterrupted!

Most of us, were not brought up to love ourselves. Our parents didn't love themselves, they were too stressed out trying to survive, and their parents certainly didn't, it was even harder for them. And what about their parents, and their parents, go back seven generations, was there ever any concept of love given? As mentioned before for some of us it was a 'spare the rod and spoil the child' kind of concept. For others it was a 'let that child cry, you'll only spoil it if you give it too much attention' I remember my mother laughingly telling me how when I was a baby she used to leave me out in the hallway alone for hours when I wouldn't stop crying. I actually think this caused me some abandonment issues which took me a long time to heal! I know I was mightily pissed off with her when she told me. I vowed I'd never do that if I had any children. And I never have done it to my children.

These are just brief examples, but what kind of pain do they teach? The teach us that violence is an acceptable way to make people do what you want them to do, and that anger and abuse are an acceptable way for us to express and inflict our own deep emotional pain on others. They teach us that we are unworthy of loving and being loved, so we end up with low self-esteem, forever after either feeling inferior or the opposite, superior to others. Low self-esteem always swings like this, you never feel equal to anyone.

I also hear so much about illnesses etc. running in families. No one ever questions it, they just blame it on the genes, but the genes are only reactors to stimuli from the environment, they switch on and off as required, according to research by Dr. Bruce Lipton in his book, 'The Biology of Belief'. A lot of people though if they look, will find that similar thought patterns and behaviours also run in families, which holistically are linked to those so called hereditary illnesses.

I've spent the past few years learning to love myself and others. I've broken the pattern of my generations by changing myself first. In doing so I've shown my children an example of a different way of being in the world. Was I afraid to change, to break out of the norm or of what I was brought up to believe was the correct way to be? Oh yes, it took enormous courage to become who I really am and to honour that integrity above all else. But in doing so, I have opened a doorway for my children to be more loving, and hopefully if they have children, they too will improve on that. In this way we raise our consciousness and create a better world for all.

Chapter 8

Managing Stress and Anxiety

'Stress, is when you wake up screaming, and you realize that you haven't fallen asleep yet'

Author Unknown

My son bought me a brilliant poster. It is called Stress Therapy and it has three circles on it. In the middle on the red section is written 'Bang Head Here' for Maximum stress and then on the white area for High Stress and on the blue area for Medium stress. I put it on the back of my door, and I can't say I haven't been tempted to use it, but so far so good! It makes me laugh when I see it!

Like most of you reading this, I've gone through many stressful occasions, I've been through marital separation, and lost my house through that, got it back, been struggling to pay the mortgage, I've experienced unemployment, self-employment, illness, anxiety, depression etc. etc. Yes, I've been there, done that, worn the t- shirt, yep!

And yes I have had my dark days in the past when I just didn't want to get out of bed and face all the hassles and dramas, and I have had the odd suicidal thought, where the illusion that it would be just better to check out now, entered my head....And I just want to say to you reading this... it doesn't have to be that way!

What I want to share with you is how I coped and how I am still coping, how you can keep the dark thoughts at bay, how you can become calm in the face of adversity, how you can perhaps even stop those low thoughts at the start before they spiral out of control and cause some form of depression. What I'm going to share with you is a tool box of techniques that I now use with my clients for Stress & Anxiety management and prevention.

If you've read this far in the book, you'll be familiar with some of this already. I've included techniques again to make it easier to follow, to save you having to leaf through pages to get to them again.

So let's begin. Stress is actually our reaction to events. When something happens that we don't want to happen, we create resistance in our body and mind to it. Our body perceives it as a threat. This triggers a stress response in the body called 'Fight or Flight'. As I said before, I like to think of it humorously as if there were a load of workmen and workwomen in our bodies having a tea break and then something happens and then it's all systems go.

Anxiety begins with a thought or feeling that has been triggered by some association to something, even if you're not aware of it. Nothing happens by itself. Everything is caused by something. Your thoughts and your feelings about yourself, and your environment can make you feel anxious. If you're a sensitive soul or an empath that can cause anxiety. Some medications release chemicals that can make you feel jittery and out of sorts. You can energetically absorb emotions of anxiousness from others too and think it's yours.

Oxygen gets pumped from the brain; it goes into the heart and lungs, to help supply more blood to the muscles in our arms and legs so that we may flee if necessary. Then adrenalin and cortisol gets pumped in excessive quantities to help improve muscle function, so if we need to fight then we have the strength to do so.

But most situations aren't like that, we're not in a fight or flight scenario, so what happens? We feel sick, our breathing becomes shallower; our heart rate speeds up, we can't think straight, we may get weakness in the legs, nausea, stomach upsets, some people think they are going to die on the spot, they may even develop a panic attack and so on.

Now that's a once off situation I've mentioned. If you are constantly stressed or feeling anxious though, what happens? Well the cortisol and adrenalin are still being pumped into your body in excess, these are natural and necessary substances that the body produces but they become harmful over a period of time when it happens continuously.

They lower our immune system. I've done a lot of research on causes of illness as I was developing a Wellness Programme for my clients a few years ago, and I have come to believe that the causes of all illness and cancers begin in our bodies when our immune system is weakened. And as mentioned earlier there is a link between the energy of trapped emotions and illness.

A person was telling me of an experience they had when they were in the middle of doing something and were suddenly seized with a sense of panic, they couldn't breathe properly, and they had pain in their chest and so on. They thought they were having a heart attack.

They were having tests to check out their heart, when they told me the story. I explained what I've said here and taught them the breathing technique. I met them again many months later. They had done as I suggested and had gotten the all clear.

If you've ever watched a nature program and have seen a gazelle being chased, you'll have noticed that they shake themselves vigorously when they are out of danger and then go back to calmly grazing? Well we humans aren't like that, and that's why we have so many health issues! We're not content that we got away we keep thinking about what could have happened.

How do you boost your immune system? There are many things you can do, including improving diet, daily use of Vitamin C Powder, nutrition, exercise, releasing negative emotions and well…stop getting stressed out! 'Oh yeah right' I can hear you say, 'How?' Well as I mentioned earlier, stress and anxiety is a response to things, it's our reactions. Life is always going to keep happening to you, don't think that you can reduce the stressful things coming at you, you won't. You might mange to deal with one and then find another comes at you, that's life!

What you can do is take on board a few of my suggestions, incorporate them into your daily routine and in a relatively short time, you will find that you feel less stressed and anxious, you will be better able to think more clearly, make better decisions, plan better and generally feel calmer and healthier over time.

I even noticed that I started getting less and less colds etc. and that by tuning into what my body was trying to tell me, that even if the symptoms of a cold were starting, that by making time to rest and relax and nourish myself, that the colds wouldn't happen. When we are stressed we feel that the world won't go on without us, yet when we then become ill we find that is has to! Look after yourself! The world can wait!

Anxiety Jump

Remember the gazelle I mentioned? If you are after getting a fright, or feel anxious or stressed, you will have a lot of cortisol and adrenalin swimming around inside your body. This makes your nervous system feel jittery and weak, it can make you feel sick. If it's appropriate to do this, find a safe place and jump up and down as fast as you can for a few moments, or dance to fast music, go for a run, or a really brisk walk. This will balance out your system again in a few minutes. Remember cortisol and adrenalin want you to be prepared to fight or flee, if you don't move and shake it off you'll probably feel awful. Or here is the breathing technique again.

Anxiety Breathing Technique

I use this every day, whether I'm stuck in traffic, or I'm stuck in a long queue, or life is not giving me what I want … I use it before I get up in the morning, before I go to sleep and throughout the day, I've been practicing this for 10 years now and it works.

Sit, stand, or lay down. Initially close your eyes, but as you get good at this you will be able to do this with eyes open. Slowly breathe in, imagine that you are breathing in from the tips of your fingers all the way up your arms to your head, chest and belly, as you practice you will be able to take longer breaths in. Then slowly exhale, imagine that you are pushing the breath out down through your legs, feet and out your toes, and that you are surrounding yourself with a feeling of calmness. Breathe out slowly and deeply. Do it a few times. Say to yourself, 'I am calm, I can handle anything. I'm relaxed.' Or if you find some resistance just repeat slowly with feeling, 'relax, relax, relax.'

* * *

What this technique does, is to tell the workpeople in your body to go take a tea break! It signals your brain to keep the oxygen where it is needed, helping you to think clearly, to concentrate more, so you can make better decisions. It stops the fight or flight reaction from triggering, it stops the over production of chemicals being secreted from your brain, and over time it improves your immune system and your health and can lower your blood pressure. You can use this technique for anyone having a panic attack also.

Affirmations / Self Hypnosis

As mentioned previously, I discovered the usefulness of affirmations a few years ago when I developed a stress related illness, through the use of them, and the other techniques I'm sharing, I got better. I discovered that they are a form of self-hypnosis and I went on to train as a Hypnotherapist. I use these with my clients as they are very effective. Basically, we have a conscious mind, this is the one we worry and stress about things with, and this part of us can only focus on seven plus or minus two things at any time.

Our Subconscious mind can focus on over 30,000 things at once and is responsible for our automatic breathing, digestion, blood flow etc. but it is also responsible for creating our reality. So in relation to stress, if you begin by telling yourself that you are calm in the face of adversity, that you can handle anything as opposed to saying to yourself I can't handle this, or I'm stressed out etc. ... then your mind will help it to become true for you. Of course if you're in the height of it and trying to say you're calm, that won't work. Use the breathing technique and reinforce it with the words I am calm, and imagine what that would feel like, then your Subconscious mind will be in alignment with your body and then you will see results.

Before you fall asleep and when you just awaken, your brain is in al-pha – theta brain wave mode. A highly suggestable state that occurs naturally. Use these times to affirm to yourself what you do want to see in your life, and allow your imagination to create the feelings you desire.

Our emotions play a huge part in all of this, so practice feeling calm. Think about how you do want to be in future situations, and put mental pictures in your mind of yourself coping in the best way you can.

Attitude

Are you a victim or a victor? Are you better or bitter? Depending on the type of attitude you adopt to what is happening in your life you can be a sufferer or a survivor. I found that by adopting a strong sur-vivor attitude that my mind suddenly started finding solutions for me. I started to think about what was the best way for me to cope, rather than feeling powerless and being picked on and having the attitude of a victim, poor me, life is happening to me and what can I do except complain, I changed all of this bit by bit, and saw that I could start happening to life instead, and although I couldn't control everything, there were still a few things I could do to improve things, no matter how small, it all added up. Survivors cope, sufferers com-plain, one gets things done, one doesn't, it's your choice.

Mindfulness

Yes here's more mindfulness again! I embraced the concept of Mindfulness and of being present in this moment now. Our conscious minds are always only focused on the past or the future. Both of these can create fear and uncertainty. We look at the past and fear it may happen again. We focus on the future and because we don't know what will happen, we fear the worst. Because we don't know what will happen, we don't know what we will do to cope, so we have to make up the worst scenarios in our heads, this leads to worry and anxiety. Because if we actually knew what was going to happen, we could then decide on a plan of action, but we can't because we don't know what will happen This would drive you nearly insane with the cycle of thoughts involved. Breaking the cycle takes a bit of time and practice. When you find yourself worrying, bring yourself back to this moment and become present in it. Are you alright now in this moment? Don't think of the past or the future, are you alright now, just now.

As you are reading this you have a choice in this NOW moment to focus on what you actually do want to happen and you can claim back your mind from worries and fears by only focusing on the best possible outcomes from now on. Seeing that you may not have the perfect life, but in this fraction of a moment you are ok. Mindfulness also means becoming aware of all you do have in your life, and practicing gratitude etc. It is powerfully life changing.

I am constantly bringing myself back into the present moment, being present more often when eating, walking, breathing, talking with people etc. A few years ago, my mind used to be always racing onto the next thing to do and the next person to see, so that I was never really there, rarely really present for anyone or anything. I also found that my mind was constantly focused on worries or fears and this made me impatient and irritable if anyone tried to interrupt those thoughts, I was caught up in the cycle of it. I discovered that when you start focusing on best possible outcomes, your mind starts finding solutions for you. No more worries or fears! Stay present in the Now! As now is the only time we can ever change anything.

Perspective

'We can't solve problems with the same kind of thinking we used when we created them' –Einstein and 'If you always do what you've always done, you'll always get what you've always got' –Henry Ford. These are two of my favourite quotes. Perspective is everything. What I believe is leading some people into depression and suicide is a limited perspective, and this is a very broad statement, please everyone don't take offence, I don't mean this personally there are many different situations out there. A perspective is your thoughts and your emotions, they can lead you down or they can lead you up.

What can happen is that we lose our jobs, our homes, our partner or run into financial difficulties etc. and we've associated this person or thing with who we are. I know I initially felt like a failure when I separated from my husband, lost my home as I couldn't stay living with him, and my job as we were sharing a business, my status was affected. I didn't feel good enough and I thought that I was viewed as a lesser being to people who knew me. In this crazy society where your worth is viewed as your possessions by many, I had identified with those things as if they were actually me.

I was too concerned with what I thought others thought of me, I have since learned that it is more important to know what I think about myself than to even contemplate what others might be thinking, that no longer concerns me now, and I don't give it any thought.

It has taken me a long time to see that I am not my job and I am not my home, and I am not my car or my possessions, so if I lose them, I still have a sense of self, of who I am without them. I won't tell you that it is easy to arrive at this inner peace, it's going to take time and work on yourself, but if you can find a sense of self that isn't your job, home, possessions etc. it will be work well done.

Why do you think some of the greatest spiritual leaders freed themselves from attachment to worldly goods? Because there is no permanent joy in those things, they can be taken from you. Happiness is actually found within yourself. If you seek for others to make you happy, what will you do when they are gone? If you are only happy when you have a job, money, possessions etc. what will you do when they are gone? This is just something for you to think about.

Thoughts

Yes some more about thoughts. I've said this a few times already, I started observing my thoughts and becoming more aware of them. What kind of things was I saying to myself? Was I being kind or critical, supportive or unsupportive? Sometimes the things we say to ourselves we wouldn't dream of saying to another. I'll ask you this, if you're not for yourself then how do you expect others to be?

I started being on my side for a change, I started saying nice things to myself, encouraging things. I mentioned already I read a great book called 'You can Heal Your Life' by Louise Hay. It helped me realize that I am not my thoughts, but that I can change the type of thoughts that I think at any time. So with my thoughts I could think the ones that made me feel good instead of thinking thoughts that made me feel bad, sad or depressed.

With practice I was even able to change feelings I was having with my thoughts. If I was feeling low, I could check in with myself and see what I was feeling, and what kind of thoughts I was thinking at that time, and I would say to myself, 'Well Paula, are those thoughts making you feel good or bad ?'

And sometimes I would allow myself to have an hour of bad feelings and thoughts, and then I would say to myself, do you feel better now? And if I didn't, which on hindsight is pretty damn obvious that I wouldn't be feeling better, I'd say well that didn't work, now try thinking better thoughts and feeling better feelings. And with practice this helped lift my moods. There's a part of us that likes us to suffer and be miserable, do acknowledge it, but don't let it take you over.

Here are the two ways of thinking again for you.

The Two Ways of Thinking

The Worst Way: Most of us are stuck in this way of thinking by default. To remain in an undesirable state of mind we have to focus on all that is going wrong or has gone wrong, keep thinking negative thoughts, have thoughts of self- blame, perceived failures, have lack of faith in the future or have negative expectations.

We have to focus on the worst that could happen, to criticize ourselves and tell ourselves things like 'I can't', 'I won't cope' and 'I doubt it', which inevitably will lead to overwhelming feelings of despair, hopelessness, fear and lack of control. We have to not accept the reality of present, past or possible future situations. We play disaster movies in our minds and can't see ourselves coping. Seem familiar?

The Best Way: To escape the cycle of undesirable states of mind, we must begin to think in a better way. The best way focuses on accepting the reality of what has or is happening, even if you don't like it, and can provide you with some new questions to ask yourself. This way focuses on finding solutions.

Ok, so I don't like what happened or what is happening, or I don't know what will happen to me, but how best can I cope with that reality, right now, where I am, with what I have ?

What is the best thing I can do right now? And if there is no action I can take, how best can I survive right now?

Can I just accept what has happened without my needing to mentally control everything, can I just accept that some things can't be changed, validated or made better?

What is going right? What do I actually have right now?

When we ask our minds the right questions, it opens the door to our subconscious mind, which has all the answers. You will find yourself picturing yourself coping in the best possible way. You will ask yourself:

'How do I want to be feeling, coping, living?'

What would that feel like?

Is there anything I can do, no matter how small, to help me feel like that now?

How can things get better than this?

How would my life be different if I wasn't depressed or having these thoughts? And could I handle that?'

* * *

Other things I did and am still doing are:

Daily Walk – Rain or shine I go for my walk, exercise gets the circulation going. Daytime walks are good as you get 90% of Vitamin D through sunlight on your skin, yes even if it's cloudy. But hey a walk is a walk, some people prefer a nighttime walk as it's the only time they have to do it, or some people do it as they feel less conspicuous, so do what works for you. I always joke about it shaking the cobwebs off me when I've been sitting around indoors for too long!

Meditation – I do this often. Even when I am walking I am meditating, focusing on my breath, my feet touching the ground, or focusing on the birds, or the trees etc. it doesn't always have to mean sitting on the floor saying OM! I never say OM actually! I meditate briefly every evening, nothing fancy, about a quarter of an hour before I sleep I focus on my breath and think about all the things I am grateful for, I connect with my angels and guides, I affirm what I do want to show up in my life, I do the same before I get up in the morning.
It sets me right for the day. I prefer to meditate in my bed with lots of warm comfy blankets. In the morning I set my alarm and in between hitting the snooze, I'm meditating. At night I'm repeating the same, without the snooze or alarm. I don't give a damn if I fall asleep in the middle of it, it works for me! Better to fall asleep with happy positive thoughts as it saturates the subconscious mind while you sleep.

Smiling – Have you noticed how few people smile, and that if you do smile, everyone wants to know why? When I started smiling, I had a pain in my face, because I wasn't used to it. Now it's the other way around. Smiling actually releases serotonin and natural endorphins, these are feel good chemicals. Your mood actually lifts when you smile. Even a fake smile creates physiological changes in the body. It helps lower your blood pressure too. Try it!

Make time for yourself – no matter whether you're working or not working, a busy mum or dad, a student or retired, you need to put aside some time for yourself, a bit of 'ME' time. A time when you won't be disturbed, where you can read a book, listen to music, go for a walk, have a bath in peace etc. Life is just too short, so find some special moments for yourself regularly and you'll find this lifts your spirits and helps you to recharge your batteries. We all need this.

Well I hope you find some of these suggestions helpful, if they aren't you can paint three circles on your door and bang your head there!

Look after yourself or your body will make you pay attention and you'll have to find the time to be ill!

How Foods Affect Moods

I shared how by changing our thoughts, we can change the way we feel, and by imagining positive mind movies we can create an easier way to see ourselves coping with whatever we want to cope with.

Now, I'd like to share what I've learnt about how foods can affect our moods and health.

When I was feeling depressed in the past, I only ate because it was a necessity to stay alive. I had no interest in cooking. I consumed mostly processed, high sugar, or fast microwavable foods. I often got bursts of energy and then a slump, which would take me ages to recover from.

Foods contain amino acids that go directly to the brain. These form chemicals that can produce positive or negative moods and affect energy levels. Dopamine is a positive brain chemical. It elevates our moods. It activates the metabolism, which helps to establish a healthy weight. It helps the brain generate the energy it needs, it stimulates the heart, regulates the flow of information through our brains, and it controls movement. Dopamine production is boosted by the consumption of foods, especially those containing the amino acid tyrosine.

Some of the foods that will make you feel good for longer are fresh organic fruits and veg, flaxseeds, free range chicken, turkey, eggs and fish (watch out for mercury) Reduce or eliminate sugary, processed or fatty foods, these stimulate acetylcholine, a negative chemical, which will make you feel bad.

Gluten or wheat in our diets cuts off the blood flow to the frontal cortex in our brain, and affects how we digest our food, which contributes to depression, concentration and digestive issues. It is also linked to the condition schizophrenia.

Some studies in the 1980's showed full or partial reversal of symptoms when some people cut out gluten and wheat, or were supplemented with a dietary supplement glycine, under test conditions! Processed gluten-free foods are not healthier for you, they have substitutes such as rice flour, potato starch and tapioca starch. These foods have high glycemic indexes, so when people eat them, their blood sugar spikes.

Our bodies are made of 70-80% water, and if we're not drinking enough water, we'll feel low moods and experience pains and fatigue. Tap water contains a lot of heavy metals, chlorine, arsenic and fluoride. The fluoride is a halogen, it competes for and displaces the body's iodine which is essential for a healthy thyroid. Clinical studies in the 1970s, based on giving fluoride as a medication, either by tablet, or a daily dose, 1 part per million, equivalent to one glass of water a day, found it could destroy the thyroid gland.

Fluoride is a neuro toxin and it suppresses the natural release of serotonin and melatonin. It contributes to issues of depression, dementia, Alzheimer's, sleep problems, arthritic type symptoms, osteoporosis, thyroid issues, low IQ, fibromyalgia and more!

I choose to eat mostly vegetarian foods. Fruits and seeds, mostly flax and chia. I've eaten chicken about four times in the last 10 years. I haven't eaten red meat in all that time. I do still like sugary foods but try to maintain a balance and have healthier foods.

I use the 80 – 20 % rule, roughly. I take Vitamin C powder, and turmeric. I drink kefir mixed with strawberries, banana and blueberries like a smoothie, I occasionally have green juice, and I'm in great health most of the time.

Wake Up to What the 'F' is in Our Water - Fluoride is a Dirty Word

Would any of us in our right minds willingly subject ourselves, or our friends or family to daily doses of arsenic, mercury, lead, aluminium or silicon?

I'm reckoning that there are a lot of 'NO WAYS' out there in response to my question.

So I have to ask you 'Then why are you allowing yourselves to be subjected to it?' Analysis from the Eastern Health Authority in Ireland found all of the above and more in our tap water. Oh yes and wait a moment ... let me introduce you to Fluoride. This is not a scare tactic; I merely want to raise awareness of something that we have become so carelessly complacent about.

Fluoride is not the natural, necessary, innocent water additive that we've been led to believe is good for our teeth. It's actually a by- product of the hazardous waste industry (Aluminium and Phosphates) yes it's industrial waste. It is not legally permitted to dispose of it into our oceans or rivers by International law, as the agent in it is Hydro Fluoro Silicic Acid (H2SiF6) it is actually listed as a poison. This is also the main ingredient of rat poison and Prozac. And yes even the synthetically manufactured products that some authorities purchase for addition to our water supplies still contain arsenic. Somehow though it has become widely acceptable to dispose of it into our drinking water mmmmm???

Now some of you are probably thinking 'so what' this issue has been debated for a long number of years now and we're tired of it. Well if so, let me ask you another question. Are you sick and tired of being sick and tired? Because in all the years that our water has been fluoridated, there have been no proper health studies on the effects of prolonged exposure to this poison to actually prove it's safe.

There have however been numerous studies which findings linked Fluoridation with increased causes of Cancer, Alzheimer's disease, Dementia, Hypothyroidism, Kidney Disease, Arthritis, Bone Fractures, Neurological illnesses, IQ and learning issues in children, Dental and Skeletal Fluorosis, Depression etc. It has been proven to be an enzyme poison. As if that wasn't bad enough, Aluminium sulfate is also added to the water, and this creates a chemical reaction which allows the aluminium to cross the blood brain barrier and creates neurotoxicity in the brain. Studies into the effects of prolonged exposure to arsenic even in small doses have also shown increased links with these illnesses.

Our bodies perceive these chemicals as a threat, and the body reacts accordingly. Our cells can only either be in growth or in protection. When in protection they close off to all stimuli and basically our immune system stops functioning properly, hence this is where illness gets a hold. Search out Bruce Lipton's Biology of Perception video on you tube which explains all about this.

The reason why exposure to Fluoride over a period of time leaves us susceptible to these illnesses and more, is that it has been discovered that Fluoride accumulates in our bodies and creates functional disturbances in blood plasma, but its highest accumulations are to be found in the pineal gland. This tiny gland which is found in the brain area directly behind the eyes is essential for producing the hormone Melatonin which not only affects the onset of puberty but it also protects our body from cell damage from free radicals.

So Fluoride is actually undermining our body's natural ability to keep us disease free. And yes in my research I discovered many things that can tip this natural balance, from diet, lifestyle, negative thought patterns and perceptions, stress, other chemicals in our food, and in personal products, unresolved emotional conflicts etc. but hey why add to it unnecessarily with our drinking water. Our bodies have over 70,000 cells which are made up of up to 80% water, and in order to function properly we need to drink an approximate of eight glasses of water every day, this number rises with exercise.

Now as I mentioned previously there have been no studies on the effects of taking this basic amount, let alone has it been taken into account what happens if people drink more of it, or how we are affected when we use it in our cooking, or the fact that it gets absorbed into our body when we shower or bathe, or swim in a pool, not to mention that the foodstuffs we eat may have used water containing Fluoride in the preparation or manufacturing. Pesticides also contain Fluoride and they are sprayed on fruit and vegetables.

The beer we drink, some of the Irish bottled waters contain Fluoride too, plus mouth rinses and toothpastes. These products contain enough fluoride to kill a child under nine years of age if ingested. (Approx. 1000 – 1500 parts per million of fluoride, compare this to 1 part per million which is in every glass of water, and which has been proven to cause illness) And even though we don't deliberately swallow the toothpaste or rinses, it actually seeps into the body through our Salvia. Under the tongue is a quick entry into the body for medication, for example, ask anyone who has had to take drops or had to put an aspirin there, the effects are quick.

I have also found some research regarding the effects of Aluminium on Alzheimer's disease which I need to bring your awareness to as Aluminium Sulphate is also in our water. Aluminium toothpaste tubes actually leach aluminium into the toothpaste and while some tubes are now plastic, you need to be aware of this. Also Aluminium cookware leaches aluminium into foods and water. This is quoted from a report called 'Fluoride in Drinking Water Increases Toxicity of Aluminium' 'Fluoridation will result in aluminium fluoride complexes which will enhance neurotoxicity or that fluoride itself will enhance uptake and synergise the toxicity of the aluminium'

It has also been discovered that using Fluoridated water in aluminium pots when boiling water actually and alarmingly leaches approx. 200 parts per million of aluminium into the water in just 10 minutes. Prolonged boiling created 600 parts per million. No leaching was found when non fluoridated water was used. A point to note also, is that some kettles have aluminium elements in them.

Fluoridation in the water has also been linked with depression as it affects those parts of our brains. Declan Waugh has written a report titled 'Human Toxicity, Environmental Impact and Legal Implications of Water Fluoridation', in which he discusses the links with depression. He presented his findings to Bandon Town Council, Co. Cork, on May 8th 2012, and there was a unanimous vote to review Fluoridation. Declan's report also successfully raised enough awareness in some American states recently, enough for them to stop Fluoridating the water until some proper safety studies have been carried out.

There is a warning on the toothpaste boxes not to swallow, and that even a pea sized amount should be considered an emergency, luckily most children vomit automatically when they do swallow it. However the equivalent of that pea sized amount of toothpaste with Fluoride can be found approximately in every glass of water we digest. Although it could be more, how do we know exactly?

It's time to wake up to the fact that not is all as it seems. Since the 1960's here in Ireland we have been programmed to believe that Fluoride in our water was a good thing to have. We were told it was good for our teeth and that it would prevent tooth decay. Studies have shown that there is no need to ingest Fluoride, as it works topically not systemically. Dr William Hirzy, Vice President of the EPA Union says in relation to Fluoride 'If you want to prevent sunburn you don't drink suntan lotion, you put it on your skin, and so if you want to have the benefits of Fluoride and oral health, what you do is put it on the surface of the tooth and not drink it'

And this is perfectly logical is it not? There is no need to expose our delicate organs and tissues to this poison, we can simply use toothpaste or rinses, and they are readily available nowadays. Studies in countries with Fluoridation vs. those with none have shown very little difference in tooth decay, with both showing evidence of general trends of improvement. However in Fluoridated areas, there was a higher incidence of Dental Fluorosis plus those illnesses I mentioned.

So that's hardly a good reason to subject us to this daily concoction of chemicals now is it? We are grown-ups. Can we not be trusted to be responsible for our own teeth? How can we allow this to continue to happen without our consent? It's time to wake up folks!

I myself was oblivious to what Fluoride actually meant, as I constantly sought out products that contained it, feeling reassured, thinking I was doing the best for myself and my young family over the years. It was only in 2012 as I was researching the causes of illness for a Wellness Programme I was developing, that I realized the importance of water for our body's optimum health. Dehydration can cause joint pains, heart palpitations etc.

So, I being in fairly good health but with an underlying thyroid condition (I was diagnosed with Hypothyroidism in 2002) decided to have eight glasses daily, I had a Brita filter but this doesn't remove Fluoride. Within a week I had developed a rash on my face, and my skin had become very dry and itchy, I had severe palpitations, fatigue and I wasn't feeling the best. It was as I was wondering what had caused this that I came across the Fluoride information which I'm sharing with you now.

As I mentioned already in another section. In my research I discovered that Fluoride can worsen existing conditions, as it was used in the 1970's to regulate Hyperthyroidism. They discontinued using it as a medication (i.e. one glass of water, a fluoride tablet or they would prescribe a bath, equal to one weeks supply!) as it was proved to actually destroy the Thyroid gland! The quantities of Fluoride that were dispensed are approximately equal to what we drink in every glass of water, 1 part per million) No wonder I wasn't feeling well! After a week of drinking non fluoridated bottled water, I was back to feeling ok again.

The following are waters that are claimed to be safe from fluoride: Volvic, Evian, Vittale, Willow Water, Tipperary Water, Perthshire Still, Highland Spring and Askbeck from Tesco – these are the ones I used mostly. I began cooking with them etc. I gradually replaced my toothpastes and rinse for non- fluoridated ones, Sarakan and Jason, being my favourite from my local health food shop. I gave up drinking tea, as it has very high natural fluoride content, it has been linked to symptoms of arthritis, and fused vertebrae and bone spurs. I drink herbal teas instead.

I eventually got a fluoride removal reverse osmosis system installed from EWT, based in Ireland. I'm in very good health now. I was originally on 200 mcg of Eltroxin for my Thyroid, back in 2002, which decreased over the years. I'm now on 25mcg every day I have no symptoms and I'm working on eliminating the medication eventually. I get regular blood tests to verify.

Despite the fact that 98% of European countries have rejected Fluoridation as being unsafe for health, Ireland continues to fluoridate its water. We have the highest levels in Europe. Irelands Fluoridation is 71% Great Brittan's is 10% and Northern Ireland is 0% Most of European counterparts like Germany and France don't fluoridate. But we think we know better do we? How long more are we going to allow it?

And if this isn't enough to make you question this policy, I have it from Declan Waugh that the annual expenditure is in excess of 15 million euro, 4 million on the chemicals alone to put this unnecessary poison into our water. We need to ask ourselves if the government are really that concerned about the health of our teeth, or do they gain anything by accepting industrial waste from other countries who can't legally dispose of it themselves?

Please contact your local TDs, join a local pressure group, sign a petition, do something for the sake of yourself, your family, your friends, your grandchildren, but please, please, stop being complacent. Let's get our voices heard. We deserve to have 'poison free' drinking water. It's bad enough that they want to charge for it, but are you going to pay for poison? I know I'm not.

Change doesn't start with the other person; it starts with each one of us. While we are waiting in the hope of having clean water I recommend that you start reducing your Fluoride intake, not all toothpastes are required to list all their ingredients, but if you see a warning notice to seek help if swallowed then you will know it has Fluoride in it.

Ask your local pharmacy and health stores for Fluoride free products. Drink non fluoridated bottled water or get a system installed. Don't use aluminium cookware with Fluoridated water. Having a bath gives your body one weeks supply of fluoride in one go, have less or shower instead! Reduce or eliminate tea, green teas etc. Try herbal instead.

Don't take my word for it, do some research, you'll see loads of articles and videos from both sides, make up your own mind. I'm writing from my experience, but yours might be different and that's ok too.

Creating Wellness

'The concept of total wellness recognizes that our every thought, word, and behaviour affects our greater health and well-being. And we, in turn, are affected not only emotionally but also physically and spiritually'

Greg Anderson

For most of my early life, I was an avid hypochondriac. Long before the arrival of the internet made this hobby easy, I had a fine collection of medical reference books, and as soon as a symptom appeared, I would be busy searching to find out what I had.

As a young child I was frequently ill. Every Christmas I missed enjoying my school holidays and Christmas dinner due to stomach issues. Then as I got older I developed regular chest infections. Before long I was having mysterious various illness, which I later found out were psychosomatic, but no one mentioned that.

By the time I was 38, I was walking around with one foot in the grave. Wishing for a hasty demise but with a guilt trip about my young children. I thought my life was over. I was married to an emotionally abusive and emotionally unavailable man, I had a house, a part time job and I'd given up anything that was fun, I'd even given up the drawing and painting that I used to love to do. The truth was, I'd already died inside.

The frequent colds and chest infections continued, then I added a thyroid illness, then regular monthly migraine headaches. As a family we experienced a lot of stress, things were difficult financially, then my son was bullied by a school principal, we got ostracized for complaining, we tried to move home, contracts kept falling through, and finally we got a house, and then my husband wouldn't let up on his verbally abusing me. Then the tipping point came.

I started to get severe headaches more frequently. I had really feared it was a tumour. Then a variety of things including severe fatigue, chronic pain, tremor, palpitations, weakness in legs and arms, short term memory loss, I even experienced a kind of lock jaw on some occasions. My mind had a kind of brain fog, simple things I used to do became a huge effort for me. I had a flat pack of a wardrobe to be made up sitting on my floor for ages, I had made up all the other furniture in my home that way, but I couldn't figure it out at that time. My niece had given me her old car, it was newer and better than the one I was driving, it took me weeks to be able to go outside and figure out how to reverse it. Sounds ridiculous but that's how hard things were for me. My blood developed a clotting issue.

I was referred to a neurologist, but he dismissed me as just having migraine attacks and tried to prescribe me an anti-depressant. I felt like he didn't take me serious. I went home feeling like an old neurotic woman. So I sought out another opinion.

My hypochondriac self was convinced I had MS or Lupus. The internet agreed with me. I began to keep a daily diary, I needed to be sure I wasn't imagining it.

The second neurologist was very kind and took time to listen to me, which was a very healing experience for me. I came out with a realization that the stark reality of my life was that no one had ever really taken the time to listen to me before in that way. It was profound.

The test results came back. The bone scans said I was prematurely aging (I looked 10 years older than I do now) my brain looked like that of an elderly patient. There was one legion. It looked like I could be on the path to developing epilepsy. I had signs of arthritis. My blood wasn't clotting properly, so I couldn't get the lumbar puncture to confirm if it was MS. The neurologist was considering it to be possibly Lupus.

And then right bang in the middle of all of this, I had a crazy thought, that somehow I may have created this illness in some way. The word psychosomatic came into my mind, so I went searching for information. What did that mean? Apparently it meant: of a physical illness or other condition caused or aggravated by a mental factor such as internal conflict or stress. At least the hypochondriac part of myself that wanted to find information was still alive and kicking!

I told someone about this and they said casually, 'So it's all in your head then?' I felt worse after that and did some more researching.

Most illnesses, possibly 90 % of them are psychosomatic. No its not all in your head, it's a mix of those thoughts you have about things, the emotions that those thoughts conjure up, and the energy of those emotions that get trapped in your body at their weakest place. I mentioned Dr Bradley Nelson and The Emotion Code earlier. He and his patients were shocked to find that when he was releasing trapped emotions, that most of them were concentrated in the areas where his patients had cancer, severe pain or disease for example.

But I didn't know about all this back then. I first read a book about stress, called 'I'm too busy to be Stressed', by Dr Hilary Jones. Then Louise Hay's book, 'You Can Heal Your Life' popped up in my searches, so I bought it. At this stage I actually was sick and tired of being sick and tired!

I began to practice the exercises in her book. It opened the doors then for me to read about and practice techniques of NLP, Hypnosis, Meditation and Mindfulness.

What followed was an amazing awakening in myself of how powerful we really are. Having spent most of my life feeling like a victim, feeling worthless and disempowered. I finally discovered my true self.

I kept writing my symptoms diary. Most of what I was experiencing, disappeared within three months! It took about eight months for the blood clotting issue to become normal again. I couldn't believe it!

This led me into passionately researching what causes illnesses, and into practicing everything I could, into reading and watching everything I could to keep myself healthy. And then I wanted to share that information with others. If I could do it, then maybe it could help them too.

And I'm still learning and finding out what helps people become healthy. I don't think I'll ever get bored. And no I'm not a hypochondriac anymore. I haven't needed to see a doctor in a long time, except for the repeat blood tests to check my thyroid levels.

I think there is a balance that needs to be reached in all things. If you are ill, seek professional help, go to the doctor or hospital and get checked out, do what you need to do, go on medication if you have to, then practice the other stuff. Then try to find the cause. That's how I help my health. It's a common sense approach. Some things can't be avoided, some things can't be healed. Just look after yourself and do what you can that might help. We're human.

Chapter 9

Aspects of Energy Awareness – Creating Inner Harmony

'If you want to find the secrets of the universe, think in terms of energy, frequency and vibration'

Nikola Tesla

I mentioned earlier in the section about self- esteem a little bit about energy and how we are stealing each other's energy to boost our own. I'd like to share a lot more about that here, and also how you can maintain your own energy without draining anyone. But let's start at the beginning for anyone who is not familiar with this.

Find Your Energy Field

We all have an energy field surrounding us. To detect your energy field rub your two hands together quickly, then separate them and hold them a few inches apart, facing each other. Bring them apart and closer to each other a few times until you feel a tingling, a kind of a resistance between your hands. That's your energy. You may need to practice this a few times.

Now on your own or with a partner, one of you hold out your palm and close your eyes, the other person points their index finger towards the centre of your palm, and without touching it, moves their finger in a clockwise direction in front of your palm. What do you feel? A tingling? Now swap over.

You'll need a partner for this one. Two people stand up, one of you turn your back to the other person and close your eyes. The person behind move back from the person, and then move closer without touching. The person with their back to you, notice what you feel when they move closer, try it a few times. Now the person behind move your hands towards the others back as if you were trying to push them over without touching them, the person with their back to you may sway forward. Then imagine you are pulling their energy field towards you, the person in front may sway backwards. Swap over. What were your experiences?

Every living thing has an energy field that vibrates around it, and nurtures all the aspects of its being: Energetically, physically, mentally, spiritually and emotionally. The stronger the energy field, the healthier we are on all levels. Our energy field is maintained by a constant flow of energetic life-force, in Chinese culture this is known as 'chi'. Energy fields with strong chi flow and high vibrational frequencies are healthy energy fields.

Your energy field existed before you were born and it exists after you die. Energy cannot be destroyed, it just changes form.

Our energy fields contain a blueprint of what we'll be physically. Illness appears in the energy field before it manifests in the physical. Scientists are only discovering this now. If you can keep your energy field healthy can you possibly heal, improve or reduce the chances of illness? Apparently so. Some animals even if they lose a limb, the energy field of that limb still exists and they can reproduce another, there are a few examples of this including salamanders, lizards and spiders.

Kirlian photography has shown that even if a leaf is cut in half, it still retains its full energy field. This could also explain the phantom limb syndrome in people who have limbs amputated, where they claim to still feel pain or the feeling of the limb or of it being strapped up prior to amputation. An energy clearing would possible help these people.

Energy References

Ancient Indian spiritual traditions spoke of a universal energy or 'Prana' over 5,000 years ago. Prana was the breath of life which moves through all forms and gave them life. Yogis manipulated this energy through practicing meditation, breathing exercises and physical exercises to maintain altered states of consciousness.

For the Chinese they recognized a vital energy called Chi. It contained two polar forces the yin and the yang (feminine & masculine) which when balanced created good health.

The Jewish Kabbalah calls these energies the astral light. Christian and spiritual pictures show people depicted with halos of light surrounding them. And even today you may have met spiritual people who just seem to have a glow around them.

To help simplify, everything is energy and energy doesn't die, it just changes form. There is a universal energy field and within that is our human energy field or Aura. These exist before we are born, and remain after we die, and illness will show in the aura before it manifests in physical form in our bodies.

Bruce Lipton wrote a book called 'The Biology of Belief' in it he shares his research which shows that our environment affects our energy field, which sends signals to the cells in the body to switch on or off depending on whether the information received suggests a threat. This is where autoimmune illness begins, as the immune system starts to attack itself. In some cases it is possible to reverse illness if too much damage hasn't been done.

Thoughts and emotions that are negative, fearful, angry etc. threaten the natural balance of the body. The cells will be either in a state of growth or protection. They go into a state of protection at times of anxiety or stress (stress is just your reaction and response to things you feel unable to fully control) or when there is a lot of negativity, either from yourself or from your environment.

If they are in a state of protection, then they are closed off to other necessary stimulus, they are on a work to rule basis, just doing the minimum to keep you alive. This is where the immune system gets suppressed. This is where illness gets a hold.

Universal Energy Field

'Dr. John White and Dr. Stanley Krippner list many properties of the Universal Energy Field: the UEF permeates all space, animate and inanimate objects, and connects all objects to each other; it flows from one object to another; and its density varies inversely with the distance from its source. It also follows the laws of harmonic inductance and sympathetic resonance...the

phenomenon that occurs when you strike a tuning fork and one near it will
begin to vibrate at the same frequency, giving off the same sound.'

Barbara Ann Brennan
(*Hands of Light*)

If you think of it this way the Universal Energy Field consists of all energies of all living things, every thought, every emotion, past, present and future all at once. Because everything is made up of energy, and energy never dies. It is considered that the ideas for all theories and inventions already exist in this field, and that they are just waiting for the person with the right frequency to tune in. Einstein knew this and so did Tesla. There are also several examples of people patenting the same ideas at the same time from different parts of the world.

I mentioned earlier about the competition for energy between people and how we can boost our own and drain another's energy. We do this because we do not know about the Universal Energy Field. This field has unlimited energy to offer us without harming anyone or anything. The more of us that learn how to tap into this source the more peaceful our world will be.

Meditation for Centering

Find a comfortable place to sit or lie down where you won't be disturbed. Breathe deeply and slowly. Focus on the centre of your chest (heart chakra) and imagine a warmth beginning there, imagine love light there. Now begin to imagine the beauty of the sky, the earth, the flowers, the trees, the wind, the rain, the rivers, the oceans, the birds, the animals and so on. They all have a creator which is love, and they have not forgotten that they came from love, only humans have forgotten.

We never got kicked out of the garden, we just forgot where we came from. We're still in the garden, it's just that we have a veil of duality over us so that we can't see or remember. Now imagine remembering that you are love too. Breathe in this love from all around you, breathe out love, breathe in peace and breathe out peace. You are one with all there is, all there was, and all there ever will be.

If you practice this recycling of energy, over time, you will be less inclined to need to grab anyone's energy, and you'll be able to maintain your energy in situations that previously would have drained your energy. And no, we are human, we are not invincible, we still need to recharge and withdraw from time to time. But there is an inexhaustible supply of energy waiting for you, it's just a few breaths away anytime you need it.

The Human Energy Field

The Aura

Also called the energy field or electromagnetic field. The aura is the non-physical shell or layer of energy that surrounds and interpenetrates the physical body. The aura and the specific fields of various organs such as the heart have been scientifically measured.

Chakras

Chakras are energy centres. Located along the central channel of the body from the base of the spine to the top of the head, they are whirling, wheel-like vortexes through which universal energy flows into and out of a person. The word "chakra" comes to us from the Hindu wisdom tradition but similar concepts are found in many cultures. There are seven major chakras in the ayurvedic /yogic tradition, along with numerous minor chakras. Other traditions identify different numbers of these powerful energy centres.

Sometimes energy gets stagnant around certain centres which can cause illness. My own example I developed a thyroid illness, that's a Throat Chakra issue, it represents speaking our truth, communicating openly and honesty, nurturing ourselves etc. Things I wasn't doing back then. I wasn't listened to and so I started to hide what I really felt, I didn't nurture myself, and I didn't speak up. When I began to deal with these issues, I began to heal. Yes I had to do other things too, but that was a part of it.

The Chakras also represent the 7 steps to heaven / enlightenment transformation / seven stages of consciousness.

Root Chakra: Survival, ego, looking out for self, part of the tribe.

Sacral Chakra: Relationships, balancing power, love and money, creating.

Solar Plexus Chakra: Self- Esteem, finding a sense of self that's not ego based.

Heart Chakra: Transformation, lower self meets higher self, learning to love, forgive, compassion.

Throat Chakra: Internal cohesion, speaking your truth, knowing who you are and aligning with your passion and purpose. Creative expression.

Third Eye Chakra: Making a difference, cooperating with others for mutual fulfilment and benefit.

Crown Chakra: Service, how can I help the world be a better place, how can I help others etc. through your passion and purpose.

Grounding / Cleansing / Protection

I'll begin with some detailed suggestions to give you a better understanding of it all and share a really simple suggestion which can be applied in seconds.

Grounding

Grounding is really important. We live in such a stressful world, it is so easy to become ungrounded. If you are ungrounded you may feel lightheaded, dizzy, disorientated, not able to concentrate or focus on what needs to be done, get headachy feelings, have blurred vision, feel tired, feel out of touch with reality, experience depression, anxiety, have sleep disturbances etc. If you're really ungrounded you might even begin to feel as if you might float out of your body at any moment! It will express itself in some way!

It is important to ground yourself regularly, and especially before and after doing any energy/ healing, therapy or psychic work. There is a passage of energy, up from the earth, and down from the heavens and all around us, universal energy. It's all about balance. Too much earth energy and you'll feel disconnected spiritually, too much heaven energy and you float away with the fairies!

Scientific studies have found that the earth's magnetic field fluctuates at a frequency of 7.8 – 8Hz (Schumann Waves) Healers brain waves become the same frequency and phase synchronize with Schumann Waves, when performing a healing. Their clients' brain waves will then also synchronize, balancing left and right sides of their brains.

Apparently grounding into the earth actually links you up with the magnetic field of the earth, which balances left and right hemispheres of the brain which shows a 7.8 -8Hz alpha rhythm.

Grounding can be as simple or as complex as you want to make it. Just do what feels right for you. Here is just a suggestion of how you can do it.

Walk barefoot when you can around your home or on grass, or sand etc.

You can set your intention, 'I am going to ground myself now. I ask that this be for the highest greater good' You can ask the assistance of the Angels, Guides, God, Spirit, Higher Self etc. or just state the intention. Imagine love light coming from above, or imagine that you are a tree, whatever feels right for you, imagine the love light traveling down your body, trunk if you're a tree! And out your feet, roots, or base chakra into the earth. Reaching deep, deeper and deeper into the earth, down to the core and connecting with that earth energy.

You may feel your tummy, sacral chakra, tan tien getting warm. Draw that energy up your body slowly, feel yourself being more grounded, bring it right up to your head, then imagine the love light from above running back down to the earth, slowly down your body connecting again with earth. Feel the heat, then bring the earth energy back up slowly, then the heaven energy back down, connect once more. Say now 'I am grounded for the higher greater good thank you'.

Cleansing

Cleansing we take a lot of others energy into our field of energy and if we don't clear it, we'll carry it with us, it's important to clear that energy before and after healing work, or after being with people that drain us etc. If you find yourself incessantly thinking of someone then they have your energy. You'll know what makes you feel off, you'll know what makes you feel good.

People who don't clear or cleanse their energy fields, can tend to find they have weight issues, or emotional issues, feel scattered, are prone to addictions or have sleep problems etc. This can apply to work and home areas too. You can have a build-up of energy in a place where people meet. For example have you ever felt a sense of awe when walking into a church or a monastery for example? Or the opposite. Have you ever walked into a room and got this terrible feeling that something wasn't quite right there, a bad atmosphere? Energy builds up over time and can affect you and others.

Again this can be as simple or as complex as you want it to be, just set your intention 'I am cleansing /clearing my energy field of any excess energy or psychic debris, for the higher greater good' you can ask the assistance of Angels, Guides, God, Spirit, Higher Self etc. or just state the intention, You can imagine that any excess energy is being cleared, anything that does not serve you. Ask that this excess energy be purified and recycled.

Now say 'My energy field is now cleared of any excess energy that does not serve me, for the higher greater good now, thank you'

You can clear the energy field of a room or building that you are in, or you can send forth a remote clearing if you are going someplace. I do this all the time. If for some reason I didn't and find myself where the energy feels off, I begin quietly to clear and protect all where I am.

Here's the above suggestion altered for a room clearing.

'I am cleansing /clearing the room or building of any excess energy or psychic debris, for the higher greater good' you can ask the assistance of Angels, Guides, God, Spirit, Higher Self etc. or just state the intention, You can imagine any excess energy being cleared, anything that does not serve you or others. Ask that this excess energy be purified and recycled. Now say 'This room or building is now cleared of any excess energy that does not serve me or us, for the higher greater good now, thank you'

Just an important suggestion here. When clearing energy its best to just consider it as excess energy rather than it being 'dirty' or 'negative', even though it may very much feel like that. A story of interest caught my eye a few years ago, when a Qi Gong healer told of how he used to throw the negative energy he had cleared from himself and from clients into a plant in his room. The plant subsequently died and that scared the life out of him, so he quit his healing work until he found out about the power of intention and how naming things carries its own energetic influences. Later on he started recycling the energy instead. No plants were harmed since!

If you think this is whacky check out Dr Masaru Emoto's research on water, consciousness and intent. He did a lot of studies by placing containers of water with words like hate, love, anger, gratitude, and some with positive images, some with negative images, he exposed some to different types of music. The results were astounding. He froze the water and then examined it in crystalized form. The water was in beautiful geometric designs when it had positive exposures, and didn't have those patterns when exposed to negative images, words and music.

Other people have done tests on rice in jars, which rotted quicker with negative stimulus. Plants that were subjected to positive words etc. have grown quicker than those that weren't subjected to this stimulus.

We humans are apparently 80% water do we need to ask what the effect of being in an environment that is negative does to us?

Protection

Protection is important because we need to conserve our own energy so that that we don't take on energetic debris from others or get affected by unwanted spiritual interference.

It's really important to come at this from a place of love, not fear. When I began my spiritual work, I was told to protect myself, I didn't want to question too deeply as to what I was possibly protecting myself from. I'd had various experiences in my earlier years, some a bit scary. I realized as time passed though that a light attracts many things. When you begin to shine some things may want to dim your shine for various reasons. It is your fear that will attract things, like attracts like energy. And of course I was in a state of fear for many years, until I freed myself of its grip.

Psychic Attack

I grew up in a house that had an awful energy in it. Besides from the feelings of depression my family had, and my brother's mental illness, there was something else there. I didn't know what it was but I always felt uneasy, it felt like I was being watched. I heard knocks on the sitting room door one night, but there was no one there, my sister was in bed one night and the door was pushed open suddenly. She saw an old man in the corner of the room. My mum would hear footsteps across the landing upstairs, there were a few things like that. A week before we left my mum told us that a man had died in the hall, when the house had been owned by a grocer. He lay in the hall for a month after falling, no one heard him and he starved to death. That was the longest week I ever had to spend anywhere!

This made me aware and sensitive to energies. The next house didn't have that energy. But when I moved out to live in bedsits, I would feel different energies, and would only live in places that felt ok to me. Of course I didn't know anything about energy then or psychic attack. Like a lot of people I had watched movies like the Exorcist that frightened the bejaysus out of me. These kinds of movies affect your consciousness, they place a fear inside of you that something outside of you can harm you, and that you are powerless. They also portray people fighting off the attacks with a cross. So this is what was in my mind about things like that. I was scared and powerless, and tried not to think about things like that.

One night though I awoke from a dream, there was this horrible roaring noise like a very loud washing machine spinning or something like that. There was a dark presence, a masculine energy, and it was pushing itself down on me, trying to smother me. I was paralyzed, I couldn't move, and I could feel the weight of it. I was absolutely terrified, but I fully awoke with my arms in the cross shape, stiffly pushing into my chest.

I had a few more dreams where I was paralyzed with fear and had that roaring noise again, but nothing like the presence again until a bit later on.

A good few times I felt a presence, but not all bad. A long time before my mum died she had said jokingly to myself and my younger sister that when she died she would come back and haunt my dad, as they didn't get on with each other for many, many years.

On the night she died, we were in a room above her room, and there was a lot of knocking downstairs. We went down, but there was no one there. Then we went back up to my dad's room. We were all having a drink and a chat. His door kept opening. Then the cat came in and went berserk, crying and looking up into all the four corners of the room. I could see my dad was getting scared. Then I felt someone hugging me as if they were beside me and putting their arm around me, and I laughed to my sister, she felt it too, we both said, 'that was mam!'

Many years later when I began my spiritual practice, sometimes I would feel something in my room, it freaked me out a little. Then I had a few experiences of waking up choking, like there was something on me like the one I experienced a long time ago. I was still in the fear mode, but I knew holding a cross up would not help, so I started researching psychic attack. Finally I came to the realization that fear attracts fear. Most of us project this false sense of bravado, inside we're like jelly though.

I was talking about this kind of thing one time among some people I know and one of them told me of an experience they kept having which was very similar to one that I'd experienced. So I shared the following with them, and they came back to me and told me it had worked and that they weren't being bothered anymore. If you do feel that something is a bit odd, centre yourself with slow steady breathing like I've shared earlier in the breathing technique, and the centering meditation. Focus on the centre of your chest and feel warmth and love light emanating from your centre. Think of love, and send love out from you, not to change anything, we're not into interfering with free will.

You can also surround yourself with the pure white light of the SourceLight. I've taken this from the book, 'Remembering Who You Are' by Laura Livingston Huff, M.S. I had the great pleasure of meeting with this lady back in 2017, when she met me for lunch in Blessington where I live.

'The pure White Light of the SourceLight surrounds me.
Only my highest good can come to me.
And only my highest good shall go from me.
I am in the Light, and the Light is in me.
I am the Light. All is the Light.
And for this I give great thanks.
Aho!'

Of course you have to get yourself to a place where what you are saying is the truth. There's no point in rattling off stuff that you don't really feel is true. You must know it in your heart. Practice it until you get the feeling.

Like energy attracts like energy. If you have fear you will attract things that make you fearful. I mentioned a video earlier about what a Shaman sees in a mental hospital. Some Shaman can see dark energies that hang around people and feed off their fear, guilt, anger, grief and so on. If you centre yourself, and stay mostly positive, they can't hang around for too long. If you learn to know your own power you can even see this as a kind of game and decide to make it inhospitable for Klingons either the etheric or the human variety to feed off you! These parasites will bring you thoughts and feelings of a negative, fearful nature. If you feel off just centre yourself.

Think of it this way, everything originates from the source, even the fallen or dark ones if they exist. If there is something that you consider bad or unaware, or a spirit bothering you, it is because it has forgotten where it came from. Your love won't change it if it doesn't want to remember, but it won't resonate with love energy, and it won't want to hang around the vibration of love energy, because it feeds on your fear. You may help it remember, or you may not. People are like this also. Be as loving as you can be, and those really negative energies or people won't be able to stay around, you'll just piss them off. They don't want to be reminded of love, it makes them feel uncomfortable, and they'll think you want something from them.

Human Psychic Attack

Of course it's not always some dark energy that's bothering you thankfully. It can be someone whom you've had a disagreement with, or someone who is jealous of you for example. Look up you tube for a lot of videos about this.

Remember everything is energy, and I mentioned earlier how we can affect others energy with our thoughts. I had two experiences of this. I mentioned previously that I know that if I feel off whether it's my energy or someone else's. A while back I shared something personal and confidential about something that had happened to me a few years ago, with someone and the next day I started to feel ill. I tested myself using the Emotion Code and according to the answers my subconscious mind gave me, I was absorbing energy from the person I had spoken with. It was negative energy towards me. So I cleared it, and asked them were they judging me, they said no, so I left it at that and felt no more illness.

A few days later I began to feel really ill. Now I haven't been really ill in 10 years, but this was bad. I felt really weak, and felt like I was losing the will to live. Again I managed to feebly get up and do the Emotion Code on myself. I checked and again I was absorbing negative emotions that were directed towards me, not by the person previously, but someone we both knew.

I was really upset I have to admit. But I realized that some people are not aware of energy or how thoughts and emotions if strong enough can affect other people. So I cleared the emotions again and sent love and light. I felt better within a day, but still felt weak. I had to do a good bit of clearing on this one.

It happened a few times after that, all from the same person. I didn't get ill again, but I could feel the weakness and recognized the energy. So I kept clearing. Eventually I spoke with them, they didn't understand but then it stopped. I'm not saying that those people were aware of having harmful thoughts towards me, and I can't prove it. I just know from researching this sort of thing, that I'm not the only one who has experienced it.

By doing the Emotion Code I realized that I must have some energetic resonance with those emotions in order to attract them to me, so I did a lot more work on myself. Now some of those emotions weren't from this life time, but they were still attracting experiences in this life time. Yes I know this is way out there for some of you. But I can only speak from my experiences. So if you're not feeling well this is just something else to think about. that might be contributing to the cause of it.

So what I discovered is that you can ground, cleanse and protect yourself, but if you still have an energy resonance with something negative, you will attract that in some form until you clear it.

So to protect yourself, keep it as simple as you like, here is just a suggestion 'My energy field is being protected now' you can call the assistance of Arch Angel Michael, your Guides, or God, or Spirit, or Higher Self, or just state the intention. You can imagine a cloak, or a golden, or violet light surrounding you, a shield of some kind, but don't send anything negative back to anything or anybody, transmute it to love. Know that you are protected and that nothing can enter the force field of your body, mind or consciousness without divine permission and that if anything tries to, that it will be returned to sender in the form of love, so that no harm or karma be created. Say 'I am now protected for the higher greater good and I am very grateful'

You can make it all even simpler by saying 'I am now grounded, cleansed and protected, thank you' once you have an idea of what it all means, which is why I've left this bit this last. By briefly imagining yourself with roots going into the earth, then all excess energy being removed and then a shield of protection surrounding you.

My daily habit is to wake up and ground, cleanse and protect my energy, if I need to do this again during the day, if I've been out and about and feel a bit off, I'll do it, and I do it every evening before I sleep. If I'm doing a healing session I do it again before and after. Generally I try my best to keep my vibration to love or above most of the time, if I feel off, I reinforce this.

The more you practice this the more automatic it is. Initially you might think it's a pain in the ass, but after a while, you'll realize that regular practice will keep your energy at a level that you want it to be, instead of being thrown all over the place by whatever other people or life throws at you.

Here's a meditation script that includes, grounding, clearing and protection. Feel free to record yourself reading this and then play it, you can use something like Audacity and add your own music in the background. Or get a friend to read it out to you slowly.

Meditation for Grounding, Cleansing & Protection

Find a comfortable place to lie or sit down, grab a blanket if necessary. Don't try to drive or use machinery while listening to this. Close your eyes, make sure you are comfortable, move around if you have to, and breathe in and out slowly and deeply a few times.

Feel your body relaxing. Breathing relaxation down into your feet, relax your feet, relax, breathing relaxation into your legs, relax your legs, relax, breathing relaxation into your hips, relax your hips, relax, breathing relaxation into your torso and back, relax your torso and back, relax, breathing relaxation into your hands and arms, relax your hands and arms, relax, breathing relaxation into your shoulders and neck, relax your shoulders and neck, relax, breathing relaxation into your head, let your jaw relax, relax your head and jaw, relax, breathing relaxation into your mind, relax your mind, relax, now all your cells, all your organs relax, at any time later today when you want to feel this sense of calm, all you have to do is close your eyes, breathe deeply a few times and say the word relax, and your body and mind will respond automatically when appropriate.

Set your intention, 'I am going to ground myself now. I ask that this be for the highest greater good' You can ask the assistance of Angels, Guides God, Spirit, Higher Self etc. or just state the intention. Imagine love light coming from above, or imagine that you are a tree, whatever feels right for you, imagine the love light traveling down your body, trunk if you're a tree! And out your feet, roots, or base chakra into the earth. Reaching deep, deeper and deeper into the earth, down to the core and connecting with that earth energy.

You may feel your tummy, sacral chakra, tan tien getting warm. Draw that energy up your body slowly, feel yourself being more grounded, bring it right up to your head, then imagine the love light from above running back down to the earth, slowly down your body connecting again with earth. Feel the heat, then bring the earth energy back up slowly, then the heaven energy back down, connect once more. Say now 'I am grounded for the higher greater good thank you.'

'I am cleansing /clearing my energy field and the room or building of any excess energy or psychic debris, for the higher greater good' you can ask the assistance of Angels, Guides, God, Spirit, Higher Self etc. or just state the intention, You can imagine any excess energy being cleared, anything that does not serve you or others. Ask that this excess energy be purified and recycled. Clearing and cleansing your energy field.

Now say 'My energy field and room or building is now cleared of any excess energy that does not serve me or us, for the higher greater good now, thank you.'

'My energy field is being protected now' you can call the assistance of Arch Angel Michael, or God, Guides, Spirit, or Higher Self, or just state the intention. You can imagine a cloak, a shield, or a golden, or violet light surrounding you. Don't send anything negative back to anything or anybody, transmute it to love. Know that you are protected and that nothing can enter the force field of your body or mind without divine permission and that if anything tries to, that it will be returned to sender in the form of love, so that no harm or karma be created. Say 'I am now grounded, cleansed and protected for the higher greater good and I am very grateful, thank you'

Slowly bring your awareness back into the room, feel your body on the bed, floor or chair, wriggle your fingers and toes, and when you're ready, open your eyes and smile!

Calling Back Your Energy / Dissolving Cords and Ties

Calling back your energy. We think our energy is just around our bodies and it's not. Yes we do have an energy field called an aura, and so do other living things, but we are all also connected energetically to everyone else and everything, and if your energy is scattered you may also be feeling drained, anxious, depressed and overwhelmed.

Where your thoughts and emotions are, that is where your energy is. Energy flows where attention goes! If you help people or are a therapist etc. If you find that you keep thinking about that person after the session, or after you've helped them, or just listened to them. Then they have your energy. We cannot save a drowning person by jumping in with them, we'd only be drowned ourselves, we'd throw a life raft, or row a boat out to them, we do what we can, then step away. Our energy is like that, we give it to people and situations to help, or people will take our energy from us if we are not aware. We need to save ourselves from being swamped.

We need to remember to take our energy back, to recharge ourselves. If you don't and are not aware, this can mean that you take on others energy too. Which can lead to emotional issues and imbalances or can lead us to have issues with weight gain or addictions, as we can carry stuff belonging to others in our energy field. We can take on all sorts of stuff from people around us. I even used to feel others pain as I passed them or when doing Reiki on clients. If you don't know what your normal energy is, you won't know if what you're feeling is yours or someone else's. Once you begin to practice this you'll become much more aware and be able to clear what is not yours, so that you can deal with you own stuff!

Cords & Ties

Another aspect of energy is energetic cords and ties. If you think about your energy, in terms of it being a bubble around you. As you interact with others, you and they will send out streamers into each other's energy field. These ties can be still connected even after many years. Once connected always connected. So anyone you've ever shook hands with, connected with emotionally, made love to or kissed etc. are still connected in some way. These cords can become entangled and create conflict for us, or a lack of harmony or peace of mind. It can also delay us from moving on to form new relationships etc. Holding onto items belonging to people can also contain their energy and can affect you too.

Have you ever met someone, whom on parting, you felt drained, and every time after if you see them, you want to just run away?

Well they have ties in your energy. You can stop this happening by just sending them your loving energy before they take it from you. You focus on your breath to boost yourself first. Breathe in and out very slowly and deeply a few times to centre yourself. Bless them, may they be happy, may they be well, may they be loved. They will be less draining.

On a funny note, sometimes if that person is fearful and unaware, your loving energy may cause them to polarize which means they might become a bit insecure and won't feel comfortable around you, so they'll leave you alone, they won't feel as attracted to you. They are used to taking your energy, and they're not used to having it being given to them, they won't understand what you've just done, they'll just feel a bit out of sorts.

It's kind of like a thief. What would happen if a thief broke into your house and you met them as they came in, and said here's my TV and some money, it's all I have, hope you have a nice evening? They wouldn't know what to do. There'd be no reason for them to stay in your house. Well it's the same with energy. There would be no need for that draining person to stay in your energy field as you've given them what they needed already. Yes there will always be exceptions, but generally I've found that this works.

We do no harm with this work. Karma is a very good justice system and it does come back to us at some stage. We do reap what we sow, it's a universal law of cause and effect. Remind yourself to do this after a session with clients to clear your field or after helping people. Do it after meeting someone whom on parting. If you don't feel so good as before you met. If we are mindful and aware, we can help keep our energy where we want it to be to help ourselves and others.

To call back your energy and to dissolve unhealthy cords and ties, set your intention, I am calling back my scattered energy and I'm dissolving all cords and ties that do not serve me now, and I ask that this be for the highest greater good. You can ask the assistance of Angels, God, Spirit, Guides, and Higher Self etc. or just state the intention.

Check in with your thoughts, where your thoughts are, that's where your energy is, and call your energy back to you. Send the energy that's not yours back to all people and situations, without any negativity, just be neutral. Imagine any cords or ties that might be entangled, you'll know if you have conflict with anyone or a situation, imagine them dissolving and healing, allowing for healthier connections if necessary.

Surround yourself in a cocoon of loving energy and set a boundary, do this for the other person or situation, so that their energy won't have the same effect on you. Then you'll have your energy back and will have dissolved any cords or ties that do not serve you.

Meditation for Calling Back Your Energy & Dissolving Cords & Ties

So close your eyes, make sure you are comfortable, move around if you have to, and breathe in and out slowly and deeply a few times. Feel your body relaxing, let your body find its natural level of breathing.

Set your intention 'I am going to call back my scattered energy and I'm going to dissolve all cords and ties that do not serve me now, and I ask that this be for the highest greater good' You can ask the assistance of Angels, Guides, God, Spirit, Higher Self etc. or just state the intention.

Check in where are your thoughts right now? Are they with another person or situation, are they in the past or perhaps travelling to some future scenario? Identify where your energy is right now. Call it back to you, see it coming in wisps of gold or whatever feels right for you, call it all back. Feel yourself being recharged as you become aware of your body and how you are feeling. Feel yourself being balanced. Strengthened. Feel a sense of harmony, a sense of peace. Calling it all back to you.

Imagine any cords or ties, as streamers of colours, that connect us with people or situations, past, present or future. Imagine yourself and a person or situation that you'd like to clean up ties with, face to face but separate. Imagine that there are ties connecting you both, from all the seven chakra points. Notice if they seem entangled. You might feel it, see it or just know it.

There are ties connecting you from the top of both your heads (Crown Chakra) see or feel them dissolving, now dissolving ties from your foreheads (Third Eye Chakra) now dissolving ties from your throats (Throat Chakra) now dissolving ties from the centre of your chests (Heart Chakra) now dissolving ties from above belly buttons (Solar Plexus Chakra) now dissolving ties from below belly buttons (Sacral Chakra) and now dissolving ties at the base of your spines (Base Chakra) Then dissolving any ties from your hands and your feet. Then imagine the sites where they were connected, being healed to allow for healthier connections to be made if necessary.

Then see / feel yourself surrounded by a beautiful comforting golden or your chosen colour, energy cocoon, and know that you have all your energy back to help you. Now imagine an object spinning around on the outside of your energy field, could be a rose or a symbol for example. This defines your energy boundary. Now imagine the person / situation that had your energy, and give them back their energy. Surround them in a golden cocoon or whatever colour you like.

If there's a few people or situations in your mind, that's ok, just see a few people or situations surrounded by cocoons and send a symbol around their cocoon to define what is their energy. Now send them a prayer, 'May they be happy, may they be well, may they be loved', and send yourself the prayer, 'May I be happy, may I be well, may I be loved' Ask that this be for the highest greater good, because we do no harm with this work. Say to yourself 'I now have my energy back to recharge me, and all cords and ties that do not serve me are dissolved, for the higher greater good, I am very grateful'

Slowly bring your awareness back into the room, feel your body on the floor or chair, wriggle your fingers and toes, and when you're ready, open your eyes and smile!

Chapter 10

Entrainment / Accessing Higher Power

Entrainment

Your body has a natural mechanism that synchs you with strong external rhythms.

There is a Universal law of Harmony for the purpose of conserving energy. In physics, it has been observed that there is less energy used where two objects are entrained with each other. Any two vibrating bodies will entrain their energy with each other, if exposed to each other for long enough.

Some examples of this: Pendulum clocks, they will entrain with each other, even if the pendulum is swung in different directions or speed initially, they fall into sync with each other.

Guitar strings, if you pluck a note on a string of a guitar in a room full of guitars, the same string will vibrate on the others.

Women in close proximity, i.e. Nuns or very close friends etc. will entrain their menstrual cycles, so that they happen at the same time.

A healer / therapist who carries a higher vibration will cause a client's energy to rise and entrain in sync with theirs, enabling them to feel better. So it's really important if you are a healer / therapist or you're the type of person who helps people, that you do become aware of your energy vibration, because if it's lower your client or person you're helping will feel worse leaving you, as they will entrain to your energy.

This can work in reverse, if you're not aware of your energy, you can entrain to their lower energy and feel drained. As mentioned before, some people entrain with every person they meet, and they can end up taking on a lot of energy that isn't theirs, which can lead to weight gain, addictions, health problems and emotional imbalances. Most of us aren't in sync with each other and this can be draining. People will entrain to the most dominant energy.

If you meet a difficult person, or are having a relationship conflict, by entraining or matching your breath to theirs, you will increase your understanding of each other. Or by choosing to be aware, you can decide to not entrain with them, keeping your energy higher or calmer will make it the dominant energy. If you slow your breathing down, if you have a long enough time with them, their energy will entrain with yours.

Another area where we entrain is expectations. Our thoughts are energy too. Have you ever gone to visit family or old friends or certain people and ended up acting the way you used to act, or saying things that aren't really the kind of things you'd say nowadays? It's almost like you became a different person. They seem to bring out the worst in you, the best in you, or the old you?

Well you've unconsciously entrained to their expectations of you. Have you ever met someone who told you something nice about a person, and you can't believe that is the same person they are talking about, because you've only ever seen the bad side of that person? What happens is that they entrain to your perspective of them, and they show you, what you continually expect of them. This also works with children too. Nobody can rise to low expectations! Everyone has the ability to show us either their good or their bad side.

Now we can't control the behaviour of others and we can't change others, we can only control and change our thoughts and behaviours, that's really important. But we can influence and inspire them energetically, to show us their better side a bit more, by thinking about the side of them we like the most. Now this doesn't mean you have to put up with being abused or violated. It doesn't mean we overlook bad behaviour. Do the best you can in each situation you find yourself. Walk away if you must or detach yourself emotionally or mentally. But when you are alone and away from them, this will help you find peace in your mind.

Accessing Higher Power

Each of us has access to a Higher Power, a spiritual source, cosmic or universal mind, Great Spirit, God, Goddess, or your true soul. It is a higher wisdom, love, power, a knowingness and it is within us all. We are not separate from these things. Separation is an illusion.

The most powerful gift that has been given to all of us, no matter how rich or poor, or our colour or creed, is our imagination and the power to create things in our lives, as I mentioned before our thoughts create things. Look around you, the clothes you wear, the room you're in, the chairs you sit in, the car you drive, the computer, the phones etc. all were just an idea in someone's mind first before they became a reality. Your lives also have been created in the same way. Our imagination is more powerful than we've been led to believe, for it creates our reality. All the highly successful people in the world know this. Buddha and Jesus knew this.

In Quantum Physics it has been proven that it is the observer that creates the result. How do we make sense of this? Why would we create all this pain, hassle and drama? Well we wouldn't if we were all connected to our Source, our Higher Power. For when we become aware and are connected, then right action follows from there. We know what the right thing to do is, we know how we affect others, we know we are all connected energetically, and there is no separation.

We know how to love ourselves and therefore how to love others, and there is no fear, or trying to control anyone. A lot of our emotional pain and suffering is caused because we want others to please us, and when they don't, we feel bad. We look for others to fill us up, which they can't do all the time. When we are connected to source, higher power, we fill ourselves up. People just add to our happiness, they are not the source of it, and if they move away, we still have a well within, that can nourish us. We cannot nourish others if we have not nourished ourselves first, we'll have nothing to give them.

Some of you won't believe this, but if you practice this, then come back to me and tell me what you find.

Whatever is in our present reality, we've somehow created either consciously or unconsciously. It is our beliefs and our thoughts, and these can be changed. A belief is a thought we keep thinking, over and over. If you hold a higher vision for yourself and others, energetically they will begin to live up to that higher vision or they will move out of your experience and not bother you.

Connecting with your Higher Power will enable you to design your life in the way you truly want it to be.

When we are aligned with source, higher power, we feel good inside, when we don't feel good, we are out of alignment. Use your emotions to help guide you. Use your emotional guidance system to tell you when you're on the right track.

Follow your passion, your excitement. What you love to do is a clue from your higher self.

Preparing for Meditation

You'll set your intention, 'I'm going to place my focus of attention on the higher qualities of myself and the people in my life and I ask that this be for the highest greater good.' You can ask the assistance of Angels, Guides, Evolved Souls, God, Spirit, Higher Self etc. or just state the intention.

We're going to focus on two people and ourselves, and we're going to find something nice about them to ponder on and thank them for showing us these qualities. This meditation if repeated daily will bring about results. If you keep focused on what you do want to see in others, they will have to show that to you at some stage, as long as you don't keep focusing on the unwanted behaviour. This isn't about control or manipulation. We help to raise another person's awareness energetically by doing this. Also if you're in a higher state of awareness, people may entrain to your energy, you will inspire them to act better.

In this meditation we will connect with our Higher Power and ask some questions to guide us.

Meditation for Accessing Higher Qualities and our Higher Power

So close your eyes, make sure you are comfortable, move around if you have to, and breathe in and out slowly and deeply a few times. Feel your body relaxing, let your body find its natural level of breathing. Set your intention I'm going to place my focus of attention on the higher qualities of myself and the people in my life and I ask that this be for the highest greater good. You can ask the assistance of Angels, Evolved Souls, Guides, God, Spirit, Higher Self etc. or just state the intention.

Picture or imagine someone you love or feel close to, if you don't have anyone like that, imagine the type of person you would like to have in your life. Or if the person has passed on you can still do this. Surround them in a pink bubble, feel the love you have for them, or the good feeling, or the happiness etc. Think about why you like/ liked/ or would like them. What qualities do they have? Are they kind, caring, supportive, do they spend time to listen to you, do you feel good when you are with them, have they a nice smile, do they make you laugh?

Tell them, 'I love that about you, or I loved that about you or I will love that about you. Thank you for showing me that part of you.'

Now picture someone whom you've been in conflict with or whom you don't like. What qualities do they have or that you've noticed, that you do like about them if any? What qualities would you like to see more of? Would you like them to be more kind, caring, to listen to you? Imagine them interacting with you in that way. Feel the feelings of surprise and delight, happiness, love etc. Allow the positive feeling to well up inside of you. Think about what you do like about this person now. Surround them in a pink bubble. Know that they are doing the best they can with their current level of awareness and consciousness, and when they know better, they will do better.

Tell them, 'I really like that about you. Thank you for showing me that part of you.'

Picture / imagine yourself. What qualities do you like about yourself? What qualities would you like to have or develop? Imagine loving and accepting yourself fully. Feel the love, the good feelings, joy and happiness. Imagine yourself acting in a way that makes you feel good inside. Surround yourself in a pink bubble. Know that you are doing the best you can with your current level of awareness and consciousness, and when you know better, you will do better.

Tell yourself, 'I really like those things about me. Thank you for showing me those parts of me.'

Say to yourself, 'From now on I'm going to place my focus of attention on the higher qualities of myself and the people in my life and I ask that this be for the highest greater good.'

Now we're going to access our higher power, state the intention, 'I am now connecting with my higher power, infinite love and wisdom, for the higher greater good of all.'

Place your hands on the top of your head, Crown Chakra, breathe deeply into this area, imagine it warm and glowing with violet light, say 'I honour my wisdom and insight.'

Place your hands on your Heart Chakra, centre of chest, breathe deeply into this area and imagine the colour pink or emerald green, or just feel it getting warmer. Become heart centered. Smile, think of something you love or are grateful for. See or feel the light getting brighter. Say 'I honour the Divine Love within me.' Feel it glowing and spreading out from you, filling the room, now its outside and it touching all the people you know, filling them with love and wisdom too. In this space there is only love and wisdom, there is no fear, no ego, just love. Powerful and peaceful.

Now place your hands on your Solar Plexus, above your belly button. Feel this area warm and glowing, with a shiny bright yellow light, say 'I honour the power within me.'

Now place your hands on your Sacral Chakra, below the belly button, feel and see it warm and glowing with a bright orange light. Say 'I honour my intuition.'

Now ask yourself a question, here are some suggestions. 'What do I need to know in my life right now?' You may get a word, a sentence, a symbol, higher power is only ever positive, helpful and wise. If not sure if it's your higher self or your ego, check if the answer was based in fear or love. Love is higher power, fear is ego. Ask three times if this is from your higher power if not sure.

Ask another question, 'If I wasn't afraid, what could I do, be or have in my life?'

And one more question 'What would I need to do to have a life like this?'

Now say thank you to your higher power, knowing that you can do this anytime you want, and the more you practice the stronger the connection will become.

Slowly bring your awareness back into the room, feel your body on the floor or chair, wriggle your fingers and toes, and when you're ready, open your eyes and smile!

PAULA O'SULLIVAN
Hara Line / Raising Your Vibration

According to Barbara Brennan in her book Light Emerging, we all have a Hara line. 'Hara' is defined by the Japanese as a centre of power within the belly. It is here that you set and hold your intentions, life tasks, purpose, deep spiritual purpose and incarnational purpose (what you came here to achieve in this lifetime)

If you are having problems identifying with your spiritual purpose, what you're meant to be doing in life etc. If you're constantly in conflict or attracting a lot of drama, hassle, violence, or causing it. If you feel disconnected spiritually, or disconnected to earth or fellow creatures, then your Hara line is probably off centre. Energetically this will affect a lot of areas of your life, happiness, contentment, and relationships. Which can also drain your energy.

Imagine a line starting about three and a half feet above your head. It has an inverted funnel (wide end pointing down) at the top of it and it is your GOD head. ID or Individuation Point. Our reason to incarnate, our connection to God, Higher Self, God Consciousness, Spirit, whatever it is to you. This line travels straight down through your body into the earth below you. It passes through three points on the body. The next point which is your Soul Seat, is slightly above the Heart Chakra near the Thymus. This point relates to our sacred spiritual longing and emotion.

Then the line travels to the Core Star, one and a half inches above the navel, it is our individual aspect of the divine, our inner essence, our deeper goodness, our creative energies. Then it passes to the 'tan tien', two and a half inches below navel. This is your 'will to live' centre. This is where some martial artists draw power to break concrete, and where healers can also connect to a great deal of power to regenerate the body. Then the line travels deep into the earth.

There are many techniques to align the Hara line, check out the book I mentioned by Barbara Ann Brennan, but let's just keep this simple. We can also use this visualization to help align ourselves and other people on their behalf. It's not about controlling anyone, we send the intention for their alignment for the highest greater good, and leave the rest up to the universe to resolve.

Raising Your Vibration

Quantum physics tells us that the universe is composed of pure consciousness, vibrating at various frequencies.

We are made up of different levels of energy. Mental, Spiritual, Emotional and Physical. These levels have a vibrational frequency which create an overall vibration.

There are lower and higher vibrations.

Lower vibrations: Negative emotions (fear, anger, unexpressed grief, sadness, basically anything that doesn't make you feel good) negative, disempowering thoughts, poor health, disconnection to spiritual source or awareness. Living in Ego mind (All about me) being controlling etc.

Higher vibrations: Empowering thoughts positive emotions (love, joy, happiness, forgiveness, basically anything that makes you feel good) spiritual awareness and connection, good health. Loving and being loveable. Gratitude.

Depending upon what frequency or vibration you are emitting, you will attract similar into your experiences. Law of attraction, like attracts like. You're a magnet! Raise your vibration for more harmony.

So to raise your vibration, think about the three wise monkeys, See no Evil, Hear no Evil and Speak no Evil, easier said than done, but with awareness you will see where you have a choice.

Food and water also carry higher and lower vibrations. Think of the 80 /20 rule. Have 80% Fresh foods and 20% crap if you must! Keep the balance. Drink clean non fluoridated or non-chlorinated water. Water from a Reverse Osmosis system, or some bottled waters, Volvic, Evian, Perthshire, Highland Springs, Ashbeck from Tesco, Willow Water, and Tipperary Water for example have no fluoride in them and carry a higher vibration. Dead food like meat or processed foods, have a low vibration and are acidic. Keep your body mostly alkaline for good health. Gluten affects your gut and your frontal cortex in the brain, reduce exposure. Fresh fruits and veg, seeds, green juicing etc. all have high vibrations. Free range products will be higher in vibrations than the others, but they are still dead food, so will be acidic.

Walking in nature, smiling, dancing, exercise, being creative, singing, meditating etc. will raise your vibration.

Create a sanctuary in your mind to help. Your subconscious mind doesn't know the difference between a real event and an imagined one. So we can raise our vibration by playing positive scenes in our mind, even if we can't actually go to a sanctuary in real life.

Create a sacred space at home if possible. With candles, flowers, incense, oils, crystals etc.

Read books, join a circle, and attend workshops. Link up with others who carry a higher vibration and you will raise yours by just being with them. But remember you are responsible for maintaining your own vibration, if you don't do the work you'll become one of those draining people that others would rather avoid!

Preparing for Meditation

You'll set your intention, 'I am going to align my Hara line, for the highest greater good' You can ask the assistance of Angels, Evolved Souls, Guides, God, Spirit, Higher Self etc. or just state the intention.

We're going to align ours and someone else's Hara line, and then we're going to raise our vibration by creating an inner sanctuary.

Meditation to Align Hara Line & Raise Your Vibration

So close your eyes, make sure you are comfortable, move around if you have to, and breathe in and out slowly and deeply a few times. Feel your body relaxing, let your body find its natural level of breathing.

Set your intention 'I am going to align my Hara line'. You can ask the assistance of Angels, Evolved Souls, Guides, God, Spirit, Higher Self etc. or just state the intention.

Imagine you are a tree, grounded by very thick strong roots, going deep into the earth, and your branches are reaching high into the heavens, or whatever feels right for you. As above, so below. Imagine there's now a gold shining straight line entering at the top of the funnel above your head and its travelling down your body, into your crown chakra on the top of your head and it lights it up, beautiful, warm, glowing, golden, enjoy this feeling, 'I am aligning with my Higher Self, my God Consciousness, Spirit' etc.

It reaches the Soul Seat on your chest (Thymus) and it lights it up, beautiful, warm, glowing, golden, enjoy this feeling, 'I'm aligning with my spiritual longing.'

It moves down to your Core Star above your belly button, and lights it up, beautiful, warm, glowing, golden, enjoy this feeling, 'I'm aligning with my deeper good and creative energies'

It reaches the tan tien and lights it up, beautiful, warm, glowing, golden, enjoy this feeling, 'I'm aligning with my will to live and the regeneration of my body.'

It travels down deep into the earth in a straight line. Feel the warmth when it connects. You are grounded to Earth energy. Feel the heat as it travels back up to your tan tien in a straight line back up to your core star, your soul seat, your ID point, as above, so below. Breathe down golden light and breathe up gold light or whatever feels right for you. Imagine your line is straight. Stay with this image passing energy down and up your body. Now create a short cut in your mind, and set the intention that you only have to think of a line running down your body to help you align your Hara line, for your energy to follow, just remember to connect with the earth to ground, bring the energy back up your body to the ID point and then back down to ground.

Now think of someone you'd like to help, ask permission first if its ok to do this for them, in your mind or in person, if you get a yes, imagine them standing in front of you. Ask that their line be straightened for them, for the highest greater good.

See the light entering their ID point, going straight down through and lighting up their Soul Seat (above chest) then their Core Star (above tummy) lighting up, then their tan tien (below belly button) lighting up and then the line running straight into the earth, connecting, then bringing the line back up their bodies in a straight line, tan tien, Core Star, Soul Seat, ID point, and back down, straight line into the earth, and ask that this line be straightened for them, for the highest greater good.

Now we're going to raise our vibration. Imagine a door in front of you. On the other side is your sanctuary. It can be anything you like, a room, a beach, a park, a valley, a garden, a forest etc. use your imagination to create a safe haven for you for future use. Now open the door. Walk slowly though, and notice your surroundings. It's a beautiful day. Notice the scents, the sounds. Take it all in. There is a sacredness a feeling of peace and awe in this sanctuary. Ramble around and find a comfortable place to sit or lie down.

This is a high vibration sanctuary, so anything that lowers your vibration, cannot stay in here with you. You become aware of some paper and a pen beside you. Mentally write down any worries, negative thoughts, or unexpressed emotions. Anything that is throwing you out of harmony, upsetting you or weighing you down. Know that you have been heard. When you're ready to release these low vibrations, let a bubble form around the page and allow it to take it up high into the cloudless sky and far, far away and out of sight.

Feel the relief. Release. Letting go. Feel the feelings of your vibration rise. A deep sense of inner peace and harmony, and happiness. A feeling that all is well, you can handle it. A feeling of bliss and deep love and oneness with all. A feeling of being centered, recharged, renewed. You notice a rainbow of vibrant colours surrounding you in a beautiful aura. You feel really good. You get up and walk back towards the door you came through, knowing that you can return here anytime you choose. As you get to the door you remember to ground yourself back to earth, imagining strong roots coming from your feet. Nothing can unbalance you now. Walk through the door and back to where you are sitting or lying.

Slowly bring your awareness back into the room, feel your body on the floor or chair, wriggle your fingers and toes, and when you're ready, open your eyes and smile!

Working with Angels & Archangels

I didn't know much about angels until I was introduced to Reiki by a friend in 2010. After my first experience of it things began to change for me. I began to explore about spirituality and then angels. I later became a Reiki practitioner.

Apparently there is an angelic hierarchy, beginning with elementals, devas and then angels. There are many levels of celestial beings mentioned in the bible.

There is a lovely book called 'Angel Therapy' by Denise Whichello Brown that gives a lot of helpful information and practices for connecting with angels.

I work with Angels all the time, whatever I'm doing. I call on them for divine guidance, for protection, for help with healing, grounding, cleansing, for help with forgiveness, for finding a parking spot, for help with creative ideas and solutions, for help with finances and so on.

I mostly connect to them in my mind. Sometimes I'll get an idea or a prompt, sometimes I'll see or hear something when I'm out and about or on my computer, sometimes I may see the title of a book, that answers a question or is meaningful to what I've asked for guidance on. Sometimes I'll use Angel cards.

There is never a negative message from the Angels and Archangels. I mentioned earlier about it being possible for people to hear a little voice in their minds on occasion that can bring thoughts of despair or doom and gloom, I can tell you that is definitely not from your angels.

I make time to consciously connect with my angels Michael, Gabriel, Raphael, Zadkiel, Chamuel, Uriel and many others every morning before I get up and then again before I sleep. But I know I'm connected to them always. We all are.

You can ask them anything, and there is no such thing as bothering them, they are delighted to help, but because they respect free will, you must ask for their help first. And sorry I've learned that I don't always get what I ask for, and no I'm not always receptive to what I do get, but on hindsight, it was always for the best. And sometimes they remain quiet while I learn the necessary lessons. You need patience. They're not going to fix you or heal you, as you and only you can heal or fix yourself, and that can't happen until you decide somewhere either consciously or sub consciously that you are ready for that. You don't have to create a ritual to connect with them, you can just ask. But I do like the sacredness of all things, so I do both.

I attended a guided meditation one time and we were to find a guide and get a message. I got Archangel Michael, and the message I got was unconditional love. I was suddenly flooded with this most amazing feeling that I had never felt on this earth before. Even though for most of my life I hadn't felt loved, and I certainly didn't love myself, even though I was trying to get there. In that moment I was left in no doubt that I was loved and worthy. I saw that there was nothing wrong with me, even though I had made stupid mistakes over the years, I realized that none of this mattered in the Angelic realms. I felt that there is no judgement there, just love, wisdom and guidance. It was a very powerful experience. I now invoke Archangel Michael every morning and evening and feel that feeling.

Try it for yourself. I have a video on you tube called:

'Archangel Michael Meditation for Protection & Unconditional Love', https://www.youtube.com/watch?v=QDs4OWsBu1I

Here's a shorter version.

Archangel Michael Meditation

Find a comfortable place to relax where you won't be disturbed. Use the breathing technique or your own version to relax your mind and body, and then ground yourself to connect with earth energy.

Call on Archangel Michael for your protection & a sense of unconditional love.

I ask that you place your shield of protection around me (my family, my friends, the earth etc.) so that no energies can disturb me and that nothing can enter the force field of my (our) body or mind or consciousness on any level of my being except by your Divine permission.

And that if anything tries to enter the force field or consciousness of my (our) mind or bodies that you will return it to sender in the form of love and light, 100 fold or 33 thousand gazillion times (or use your own numbers here!) so that no harm and no karma be created, for the highest greatest good of all concerned

'I ask that you fill me (us) with the love and light energy of the Christ Consciousness, I am self's permission, so that every cell, every atom of my (our) body will be filled with higher love and light and that the inner Christ Light and radiance within us which is invincible power, dissolves everything that is not Divinely planned for us right now for the higher greatest good.'

I ask that you fill me (us) with a sense of unconditional love, I ask you to connect with me and allow me to feel the feeling of unconditional love. Notice if your heart chakra (centre of chest gets warmer) notice perhaps a sense of peace. Sometimes we might see an image or get a whiff of scent or a feeling of a gentle presence. Notice if you feel anything, it's ok if you don't, you might after doing this a few times.

Know that you are loved, allow that feeling, and know that you are worthy, you are so beautiful and acceptable in the eyes of the Angels. You are enough. You always have been and you always will be. Know this to be true. You feel the feelings of being loved, accepted, respected, of being seen of being heard, you are appreciated, and valued

When you have a sense of this, share it. Send this feeling out to those nearest and dearest to you. Send it out to neighbours, send it out to strangers. People you've seen on the street. Send it out around your area, the county you live in, your part of the world. Send it out to everybody, people you like and people you don't like. People you've forgiven or maybe never will forgive (until you reach that level) this love encircles our planet, it includes all the creatures and all the beings.

Then send it to Archangel Michael and the other angels and beings that look after us and help us to raise our consciousness send it to them as a gift. Then ask Archangel Michael to help you to keep this awareness with you all the time in your energy field. Say a big thanks.

Then notice your breathing, ground yourself, and bring yourself slowly back to everyday awareness.

If we are calm and positive the Angels can bring us messages to help us.

A couple of years ago for a few weeks I kept getting a scenario in my mind as I passed a certain spot on the road. It was a scene of me crashing into a telegraph pole, and then in it I was asking my son was he ok, and then me telling him I had to do that to save us.

Now I'm really aware of my thoughts and I thought that this was one of those negative thought forms that sometimes sneak into my awareness, so I paid it no heed.

About a month after that, I was driving my son to school on the same stretch of road, time seemed to slow down, and I noticed my son was very pale with a strange look on his face. Asking him was he ok, he told me that a scene of us having a really horrible crash had come into his mind. I said oh I hope not, but I'll slow down a bit more just in case.

As we rounded a sharp corner, a car was going wildly out of control, and heading straight for us on our side of the road. I barely had time to react, so I swerved towards the ditch and crashed into a telegraph pole! I asked my son was he ok, he was, but then the car crashed right into us. We survived it. My son told me later that a fireman who had to cut my side of the car to get me out, had said to him, that me crashing into the pole had saved us, as it had taken the energy momentum, so that the other car only hit us at their speed and not the two combined.

Another time I was driving down a road and coming up to a T junction, there was a bit of a bend in the road, and I heard a voice in my mind saying slow down, so I did, as I rounded the bend a girl stepped out in front of me suddenly and crossed the road, I had enough time stop. I've had a few different things like that happen.

I spent a lot of my life feeling unsupported, but when I connected with the angels that changed for the better. Give it a go if you feel inclined to do so, see if it makes things a bit easier for you. I hope it does.

Seven Steps to Heaven

We are surrounded by reminders of the seven steps to Heaven / Enlightenment/ Transformation, but most of us are not really aware of them and how they can help us.

Step One of the seven steps to Heaven begin at Hell, in a way. It is represented by Saturn (Satan in Astrotheology) the slowest planet, the limitations of time. 'Baptism' - born into our tribe. The 'Root Chakra' – our basest survival needs, our ego, self- preservation, where we get caught up in ourselves, habits, addictions, anger, our lower selves. In Alchemy it's the Lead of self. In Energy it's the lowest frequency and vibration. It is our ancient and stubborn soul in Spirituality. By letting go of our fear and anger, by looking out for others as well as ourselves, by realizing that there is nothing outside ourselves that can harm or control us except our own vain imaginations, we get to move up to the next level.

Step Two is represented by Jupiter, the metal Tin. 'Communion' - greater interaction with others, community. 'We' rather than 'I'. The 'Sacral Chakra' – when we move up from our ego desires and fears, we find balance between love, money and the power to create. Through using mental exercises and intuition we can seek to let go of repressed feelings that are at the root of all our addictions. With more balanced emotions we go to level three.

Step Three is represented by Mars, the metal Iron. 'Confirmation' – discovering who we are in the world. The 'Solar Plexus Chakra', willpower, the will to live. When we gain insights into our behaviours and how they affect ourselves and others, we learn to assert ourselves without dominating or submitting, we find equality, personal honour, courage, and we move away from materialism and the battles it causes. Onwards and upwards.

Step Four is represented by Planet Venus, the symbol for life force, the Egyptian Ankh, denotes a circle over a cross, the triumph of spirit over matter, the metal is Copper. 'Marriage' – we become more caring and less manipulative to others. 'Heart Chakra'-we balance our emotions further, learn our lessons from love and develop greater compassion, forgiveness and empathy. We learn to give unconditionally while respecting our own boundaries. We're on the way!

Step Five is represented by Mercury and the metal Mercury. 'Confession' – power of speech. 'Throat Chakra' – speaking our truth, liberation, creativity, inspiration, expressing our thoughts but balancing speaking with listening, being aware of our inner power without getting caught in the pride of our wisdom, discovering mind over matter. Almost there!

Step Six is represented by the Moon, Silver. 'Holy Orders' – being divinely guided and sharing that knowledge to help others. 'Third Eye Chakra' – intuition, free of the ego and instinctual influences, a feeling of connectedness to everyone and everything and seeing how you play your part in affecting the world around you. Are we there yet?

Step Seven is represented by the Sun, Gold. 'Last Rites' – death to the old ways of living and being in the world. 'Crown Chakra' – transformation, a oneness with the universe in which the Divine is experienced. In Alchemy it is the Gold of self, the Philosophers Stone. It is higher consciousness, the highest vibration and frequency. We are in touch with higher guidance, knowingness, enlightenment, bliss, and can fulfil our highest potential. Ah heaven!

Your Metaphysical Mind

'Reality is merely an illusion, albeit a very persistent one.'

Albert Einstein

It took me a long time to realize this myself! Most of us live our lives day by day creating our reality through the lens of the reasoning mind and our perceptions, which causes us to feel disconnected and separate from everyone and everything else. Have you ever experienced the same situation as another person did, but on talking about your experiences, you noticed that you both had different stories to tell about the same event, causing you to wonder if you were both talking about the same thing?

We base our reality mostly on the five senses, which is like taking many pictures of the city you live in, and making up your mind about it, instead of going into the city itself. So the difference between your reasoning mind and your metaphysical mind, is that you also use other aspects like intuition, inspiration, imagination, thoughts and feelings that create a sense of connection with everything else.

Feeling connected to everything else gives us a greater sense of empathy with our world. We see that we are a part of the problems that surround us, and that we are also a part of the solution. It gives us a greater sense of responsibility for the part we play in the whole situation.

We can then become aware of another basic universal principle, that of cause and effect, you reap what you sow. Each thought we think energetically affects everything around us. If we have repeated dominant thoughts, these in time will affect our behaviour, our actions, and our habits, which will affect those people who interact with us. In turn how we affect those people, will in turn affect the people they interact with. And on it goes like a ripple effect.

Most of us are not creating our reality with any kind of awareness, we are unconsciously recreating patterns of behaviours that we perhaps learnt as children. We are on autopilot, reacting to our experiences with our different perceptions. I mentioned this throughout the book. With metaphysics we start creating consciously the kind of world we would like to experience, because with this knowledge comes the awareness that everything returns to sender at some stage. So that everything we send out there, our thoughts, emotions, actions and deeds become the script for our life's experiences.

Oh I know this may sound way out there for some of you. We haven't been programmed to think in this way. We have been brought up to believe that our power is external. It comes from other people, situations, material things etc. We were not told that we were also the co-creators of our day to day reality.

If you want to start using your metaphysical mind, begin by using your thoughts, imagination, intuition, inspiration and emotions in a more positive way. Start with the awareness that everything you think, say and do is affecting someone, somewhere. Now decide what kind of affect you want to be creating. Know that if you are the creator of hassle, drama, suffering, pain etc. for others then you are mapping out a future of misery for yourself. Your life experiences will begin to change, when you do!

Essential Toolkit

Breathing Technique

Find a place where you won't be disturbed. Make sure you're warm and comfortable. Close your eyes, uncross arms and legs. Imagine that the breath is filling your chest and belly when you are inhaling. Your belly will rise. Placing your hands on your belly will let you know when you've managed this. When you are exhaling, imagine that the breath is travelling out of your belly and down through your legs, feet and toes. Your belly will fall. Do it slowly and deeply, belly rise and fall. Do this five times or more. Breathing in calmness and relaxation, breathing out any worries or cares. Breathing in peace, breathing out love.

The Two Ways of Thinking

The Worst Way: Most of us are stuck in this way of thinking by default. To remain in an undesirable state of mind we have to focus on all that is going wrong or has gone wrong, keep thinking negative thoughts, have thoughts of self- blame, perceived failures, have lack of faith in the future or have negative expectations. We have to focus on the worst that could happen, to criticize ourselves and tell ourselves things like 'I can't', 'I won't cope' and 'I doubt it', which inevitably will lead to overwhelming feelings of despair, hopelessness, fear and lack of control. We have to not accept the reality of present, past or possible future situations. We play disaster movies in our minds and can't see ourselves coping. Seem familiar?

The Best Way: To escape the cycle of undesirable states of mind, we must begin to think in a better way. The best way focuses on accepting the reality of what has or is happening, even if you don't like it, and can provide you with some new questions to ask yourself. This way focuses on finding solutions.

Ok, so I don't like what happened or what is happening, or I don't know what will happen to me, but how best can I cope with that reality, right now, where I am, with what I have ?

What is the best thing I can do right now? And if there is no action I can take, how best can I survive right now?

Can I just accept what has happened without my needing to mentally control everything, can I just accept that some things can't be changed, validated or made better?

What is going right? What do I actually have right now?

When we ask our minds the right questions, it opens the door to our subconscious mind, which has all the answers. You will find yourself picturing yourself coping in the best possible way. You will ask yourself:

'How do I want to be feeling, coping, living?'

What would that feel like?
Is there anything I can do, no matter how small, to help me feel like that now?

How can things get better than this?

How would my life be different if I wasn't depressed or having these thoughts? And could I handle that?'

Creating Your Mind Movie

Close your eyes, imagine that you are going into your own private movie theatre, you are alone and you are perfectly safe. Find a seat. Choose a scenario that you want to be or feel better in. How do you want to see yourself acting? How do you want to feel? What do you want to look and sound like? Now look up at the screen. You notice a freeze frame of a scene with you on the screen. Now press play and practice seeing, feeling and hearing the new you. Press pause, think of anything you want to change or improve. Then rewind the movie fast, pause and play the new scene. Repeat this at least three times and then press save. This will take some time to get used to. Just keep practicing. Anytime the disaster movie or an image of what you don't want comes on in your mind, eject and play the new movie instead. Keep improving on what you want. If you can see it in your mind then you're already halfway there. When you are comfortable with what's in your mind, you can then start to practice it in your life.

Meditation for Centering

Find a comfortable place to sit or lie down where you won't be disturbed. Breathe deeply and slowly. Focus on the centre of your chest (heart chakra) and imagine a warmth beginning there, imagine love light there. Now begin to imagine the beauty of the sky, the earth, the flowers, the trees, the wind, the rain, the rivers, the oceans, the birds, the animals and so on. They all have a creator which is love, and they have not forgotten that they came from love, only humans have forgotten.

We never got kicked out of the garden, we just forgot where we came from. We're still in the garden, it's just that we have a veil of duality over us so that we can't see or remember. Now imagine remembering that you are love too. Breathe in this love from all around you, breathe out love, breathe in peace and breathe out peace. You are one with all there is, all there was, and all there ever will be.

About the Author

Paula O'Sullivan lives in Blessington, Co. Wicklow, in Ireland, with her two sons. To date she has qualified and practiced as a Hypnotherapist Reiki Practitioner & Life Coach. She is an artist, photographer and a bit of an entrepreneur. This is her second book. The first one is called 'Different Perspectives for a Different World – Essays for Life' the first print run was limited to only 200 copies. Her revised edition is now widely available. Paula is passionate about personal development and metaphysics and how it can help maintain our health, wellbeing and ease the suffering of ourselves and others.

www.paulaosullivan.com

Recommended Reading

Here are just some of the books I've read, researched or practiced stuff from that you may be interested in.

The Emotion Code by Dr Bradley Nelson

Edgar Cayce on Atlantis by Edgar Evans Cayce

Light Emerging by Barbara Ann Brennan

Hands of Light by Barbara Ann Brennan

The Power of Now Eckhart Tolle

The Law of One by Ra an humble messenger of The Law of One

The Grand Design books by Patrick Francis (Paddy McMahon)

Urban Shaman by Serge Kahili King Ph.D.

Hidden Mysteries by Joshua David Stone Ph.D.

Soul Psychology by Joshua David Stone Ph. D.

You Can Heal Your Life by Louise Hay

Five Lives Remembered by Dolores Cannon

The Three Waves of volunteers and The New Earth by Dolores Cannon

Between Life and Death by Dolores Cannon

Keepers of the Garden by Dolores Cannon

The Biology of Belief by Bruce H Lipton Ph.D.

The Honeymoon Effect by Bruce H Lipton Ph.D.

The Four Agreements by Don Miguel Ruiz

The Four Insights by Alberto Villoldo

Feeling is the Secret by Neville Goddard

The Power of Awareness by Neville Goddard

The Kybalion by The Three Initiates

The Strangest Secret by Earl Nightingale

Working with the Law by Raymond Holliwell

The Power of Your Subconscious Mind by Joseph Murphy

Teach Yourself NLP by Steve Bavister & Amanda Vickers

Codependent No More by Melodie Beattie

Feel the Fear and do it anyway by Susan Jeffers

The Complete Works of Florence Scovel Shinn by Florence Scovel Shinn

E² by Pam Grout

Many Lives, Many Masters by Dr Brian Weiss

Only Love is Real by Dr Brian Weiss

Same Soul Many Bodies by Dr Brian Weiss

Anatomy of an Illness by Norman Cousins

Head First by Norman Cousins

Quantum Love by Laura Berman

The Vortex by Esther & Jerry Hicks

Remembering Who You Are by Laura Livingston Huff, M.S.

Distant Mental Influence by William Braud, Ph. D.

Mind Reach by Russel Targ / Harold E. Puthoff

Being You Changing the World by Dr Dain Heer

Fuck it Do What You Love by John C. Parkin

Shamanic Journeying by Sandra Ingerman

Your Forces and How to Use Them by Christian D. Larson

Mastery of Self by Christian DAA Larson

Awareness by Anthony De Mello

The 7 AHA s of Highly Enlightened Souls by Mike George

Divine Magic by Doreen Virtue

Angel Medicine by Doreen Virtue

There's a Spiritual Solution to Every Problem by Wayne W. Dyer

Secrets of the Code edited by Dan Burstein

The Emerald Tablet by Dennis William Hauck

Effortless Power by Rich Morales, M.D.

Different Perspectives for a Different World –

Essays for Life (Revised Edition) by Paula O'Sullivan

Full Catastrophe Living by Jon Kabat-Zinn

The Rules of Life by Richard Templar

Creative Visualization by Shakti Gawain

Developing Intuition by Shakti Gawain

Access the Power of Your Higher Self by Elizabeth Clare Prophet

Psychic Development for Beginners by William W. Hewitt

I Can Mend Your Broken Heart by Paul Mc Kenna / Hugh Willbourn

Teach Yourself Cognitive Behaviour Therapy by Christine Wilding

What We May Be by Piero Ferruci

Spiritual Warfare - The Art of Deception by Ari Kopel

Love is letting Go of Fear by Gerald G. Jampolsky, M.D.

The 7 Habits of Highly Effective People by Stephen R. Covey

A Return to Love by Marianne Williamson

The Divine Matrix by Gregg Braden

Introduction to Tantra by Lama Yeshe

Quantum Touch by Richard Gordon

The Five Love Languages by Gary Chapman

The Celestine Prophecy by James Redfield

The Tenth Insight by James Redfield

The Secret of Shambhala by James Redfield

The Twelfth Insight by James Redfield

The Lineage of the Codes of Light by Jessie E. Ayani

The Star – Borne by Solara

The Secret by Rhonda Byrne

Angel Therapy by Denise Whichello Browne

Conversations with God by Neale Donald Walsch

I'm Too Busy to be Stressed by Dr Hilary Jones

Printed in Great Britain
by Amazon

83746737R00149